IDEAS FOR *Community* MINISTRIES

JOY LUEBBERT BOLTON

Woman's Missionary Union
Birmingham, Alabama

Woman's Missionary Union
P.O. Box 830010
Birmingham, AL 35283-0010

Cover design by Janell E. Young

Dewey Decimal Classification: 261.8
Subject Headings: CHURCH AND SOCIAL PROBLEMS
                  MISSION ACTION—HANDBOOKS,
                    MANUALS, ETC.
                  SOCIAL ACTION
                  COMMUNITY SERVICES

ISBN: 1-56309-075-9
W933108•0693•10M1

With grateful appreciation to my husband, Lee, who has endured over a year of research, a cluttered dining room table, the clatter of the printer at all hours, and who stayed home with the kids while I went on a missions trip to Rwanda, Africa, in the middle of this project. Years ago I was told that WMU stands for We Men Understand, and he is a WMUer par excellence!

CONTENTS

PROLOGUE

Have you ever wanted to live when Jesus lived in order to show Him how much you love Him? As a college student, that longing consumed my thoughts during my daily time of prayer and Bible study. I envisioned myself carrying enough water to ensure that Jesus was never thirsty as He traveled across dusty roads. And at times, I imagined staying up well into the night, long after others had fallen asleep, listening to all His teaching. But I cannot step back into history and neither can you. Instead we must learn how to answer this question ourselves: Did you ever want to live when Jesus lived in order to show Him how much you love Him? What will your answer be?

Jesus gave an example of how we could show our love for Him; and He makes it clear in Matthew 25:35-46. "The King was hungry, thirsty, a stranger, naked, sick and in prison; and the righteous ministered to him! The identity of Jesus with his people is a major New Testament teaching (cf. Acts 9:4f.; 1 Cor. 1:13; 8:12). In ministering to the needy, one ministers to Christ."[1] Our community ministry is identifying with Jesus as we minister to others.

The Bible contains a balanced message of the whole gospel for the whole person. "'Love the Lord your God with all your heart and with all your soul and with all your mind.' This is the first and greatest commandment. And the second is like it: 'Love your neighbor as yourself.' All the Law and the Prophets hang on these two commandments" (Matt. 22:37-40 NIV). It is clear that we are to be God's agents of ministry. We must learn to see through the eyes of God, to hear through the ears of God, and indeed to develop hearts that beat with the heart of God. This can happen as you act on the ideas in this book. Such action will enable you to say to Jesus: "I love You!"

Trudy Johnson

[1]Frank Stagg, "Matthew," in *Broadman Bible Commentary,* ed. Clifton J. Allen (Nashville: Broadman Press, 1969), vol. 8 , 227.

INTRODUCTION

Human need is present everywhere we turn. We are horrified by the rising rate of crime and violence in what we once thought were "safe" neighborhoods. We ache for the victims, for the abused children, and for the persons who have destroyed their own lives through drug and alcohol abuse.

We fear for our own jobs in tough economic times and wonder how we can help the unemployed and homeless. Many of us realize that we are only one or two paychecks away from homelessness ourselves and have become more compassionate toward those in dire straits. Yet we also want to do something to stop the cycle of poverty and welfare that seems to just keep repeating itself among low-income, undereducated families.

The AIDS epidemic has given rise to a new generation of "untouchables." Medical science and better health care have given us the dual blessing and curse of longer life. Living wills are becoming increasingly popular as people try to avoid being kept "alive" by machines. The right to die peacefully, supported by family and friends, has become a crusade for many through the hospice movement.

When the needs seem overwhelming and I wonder, What can one person possibly do? I am reminded of a column written by David Yeager for his church newsletter. He is pastor of the College Parkway Baptist Church, Arnold, Maryland.

> At the end of our street where the blacktop dead-ends near the tree line, there is a split-rail fence. On the other side of the fence, between the fence and the woods, is a narrow strip of land filled with tall grasses, several thorn-laden bushes, and a few mushrooms. For reasons I have yet to figure out, Sarah Martin refers to this overgrown parcel as "my backyard." Anytime we go walking or bike riding, she wants to stop at her "backyard" and check on things. She will step around the end of the fence, carefully avoiding the thorn bushes (with which she has had a few encounters), and walk along the edge of the tall grass, occasionally stopping to pick up a rock or stick or other object of interest. Not being as captivated by her "backyard" as she is, I usually just sit and wait for her to tire of her explorations. And sometimes I wait quite awhile before she is ready to leave.

> I don't know what attracts Sarah to this grassy patch, nor why she calls it her own. I just know that in her mind it is hers and she feels compelled to visit her "backyard" frequently to make sure all is well.

> I have often wondered what our world would be like if each of us would acknowledge that a portion of our community was our "backyard." Not that portion which is of self-interest to us, nor that from which we might expect some return from our investment of concern. But rather that part of our community that no one else thinks about; that some avoid due to its unattractiveness; that others ignore because of its commonness. Our "backyard" might be a child in a single parent household that needs a little extra attention. It might be an elderly person who is alone and in need of someone to talk to. It might be a family with a special needs member with whom we could spend a little time, providing a respite to the care giver.

> I suspect there are plenty of "backyards" in our community. Which one is yours?

This book is about "backyards." There are some who would try to make us feel guilty because we are not supporting in every cause, helping to solve every problem, or meeting every need. This is impossible. But tending to a "backyard" is not only doable, it is as important to our own well-being as puttering in a literal backyard.

My backyard includes a nursing home and tutoring an adult nonreader. In researching this book, I've learned about many others, and I want to share them with you. Do not feel guilty, but use these examples to find the ministry that best suits your group or you as an individual. I've met some wonderful, caring people in my search for information and insight on how to be a volunteer. I especially appreciate COVAAC (Coordinators of Volunteers of Anne Arundel County) for letting me join their group and learn about the work of a volunteer coordinator.

May God bless you richly as you tend your backyard.

Joy Bolton

THE WORLD OF COMMUNITY MINISTRY

Contrary to conventional wisdom today, volunteerism is alive and well. More people than ever before are involved in community causes that range from human needs concerns to animal welfare, from the environment to neighborhood safety, and from promoting the arts to the preservation of culture. While it is true that the number of women who do not work outside the home has shrunk dramatically, community agencies have adapted to make volunteering available to people of all ages, backgrounds, and work schedules.

The needs of our communities are larger than any one church or missions organization can meet. Therefore, in trying to minister to human need, most of us find ourselves working with various community agencies and nonprofit groups. An awareness of the agencies in your community, how they operate, and who to contact will facilitate ministry as an individual or by a group.

The purpose of this book is to introduce you to volunteerism in today's world and suggest ways that you can minister in your own community.

Volunteer Coordinators

Across the country, a network of agencies that use volunteers has been developed. In many communities, you may call a county office to learn about volunteer needs in the area. The National Volunteer Center publishes a directory of participating groups and provides literature for program directors and volunteer coordinators. Colleges are now offering courses in volunteer management. The volunteer coordinator or director has become the point of entry for many community services.

To get started in your community, first call your county to learn if there is a volunteer center or a volunteer coordinator for your area. Contact this person to ask about needs in the community and agencies that you might contact.

When you choose a group who works in your area of interest, be prepared for an interview as if you were applying for a job. In essence you are. Community organizations have a high regard for volunteers and often treat them as equals with paid staff. Volunteer coordinators know that volunteer retention is higher if they can successfully match a volunteer with a satisfying job. Community agencies have become geared to flexible schedules combined with high expectations. And people are responding!

Encouraging Community Ministry

While many churches are bemoaning the fact

that they cannot get people to participate in church-based projects anymore, others have taken the approach of affirming the ministry of the laity in the community. While leading people to be involved in ministry through the church, Woman's Missionary Union and Brotherhood need to recognize and commend the ministries performed by individuals and groups such as Sunday School classes and support groups. WMU can best serve the church and community by periodically giving recognition and encouragement to all persons in the church who are involved in community ministry.

Witnessing Through Community Ministry

Many have avoided involvement with secular or government agencies because of the commitment to combining ministry and witness. We have at times been guilty of only supporting our own Baptist ministries, and missing the many other opportunities that are available. While involvement with church and community ministries may still be our first choice, it should not be the only option.

Opportunities to witness arise naturally in the context of community ministry. Now, if you call a secular nonprofit agency to volunteer and ask, "Can I tell people about Jesus while I'm working?" the answer may very well be no. But if you approach community service with the idea of helping meet needs in the community that you could not do alone and are open to the natural occasions to share your faith, you will be able to witness even in secular ministry settings.

Here are some things to keep in mind as you prepare for community ministry either as an individual or as a group:
• What are my personal interests and skills?
• What would I like to accomplish through community ministry?
• What age group do I want to work with?
• Do I prefer to work alone or with a group?
• What kind of time commitment can I make?
• Do I want to work directly with persons in need, or would I prefer a "behind-the-scenes" ministry?

Call an agency or church-sponsored community ministry center that is involved in the type of community ministry that is of interest to you or your group. Ask about their needs and how they use volunteers. Schedule a visit with the volunteer coordinator or program director, and do not hesitate to ask these questions:
• What are the specific duties of the position?
• Who is the supervisor?
• What skills does this service require? Could I learn new skills as a volunteer?
• What could a group do on a one-time basis? Ongoing basis? How do I schedule a group project?

There are many avenues of service. Don't be discouraged if you are the only one in your group who wants to do community ministry. Go ahead and find your niche. Report regularly to your church or women's group about the community service in which you are involved. If group projects are difficult, but several in your group are involved in different volunteer ministries, have them share regularly. A group project may very well develop as others take interest in what one person is doing or as she shares a specific need that has come up in her work.

Bill Viel, director of Inner Harbor Ministry in Baltimore, Maryland, identified the following as most important for individuals or groups to know about ministry:

1. There is something for everyone to do.
2. Behind-the-scenes volunteering is just as important as those in leadership or directing each ministry.
3. Professionalism is not required in most ministries. Commitment is a priority.
4. Be flexible and open to God's leading as He shows you needs.

A volunteer coordinator, a Baptist center director, an associational church and community ministries director, or a special ministries missionary is waiting for your call!

A SPECIAL WORD
Many of the ideas in this book suggest working with existing community agencies or church-sponsored ministries. Some towns or counties may not have community agencies or existing programs. The ministry ideas in this book can be done by individuals or groups working on their own. As you read this book, identify needs, secure resources, develop skills, and lead out in doing ministry in your town or city.

GETTING OTHERS INVOLVED IN COMMUNITY MINISTRY

Community ministry is not a simple task. Although many of the helping things we do are in and of themselves just small kindnesses extended along the way, being in the right place at the right time often takes some planning. This becomes even more important when working with others.

Planning

To have successful ministry projects and ongoing service opportunities, objectives and goals, good planning, participation, and evaluation are necessary. Involve others in seeing the need and dreaming the dream. Use a ministry plan sheet (see sample on p. 68) to guide you in covering all the details. Be sure everyone involved in planning has a specific assignment that is worthwhile and contributes to the success of the projects. Get feedback about assignments and try to use people in the places where they feel most comfortable. How each person feels about her assignment is very important to the success of the project.

Service Expectations

Before inviting others to participate, be sure you know exactly what needs to be done. Develop one or several service expectations lists, depending on what needs to be done. Include simple routine needs as well as very challenging work. Some people will prefer the more basic tasks, but others respond only to challenges.

Many people have become frustrated by the lack

of response to a general appeal such as, "We need help with prison ministry." You later hear them complaining, "Nobody cares." Be specific: "We need four people to go to the prison on Thursday evenings from 7:00 to 8:30 to teach Spanish." Or, "We need boxed cards, stationery, and stamps for the prison chaplain to give to prisoners when he visits."

Each of these requests is specific. Each supports prison ministry. The second can even be done by someone who is concerned but cannot go to the prison regularly.

Skills Survey

Specific skills may be needed for some ministry projects. A skills survey will help you build a pool of available persons and will help you match the need with the person best able to complete the task.

Use the skills survey found at the back of this book. Get every youth and adult you can find to complete it. Explain that everyone has skills that are useful in community ministry. However, we may overlook them. The survey is useful for identifying or uncovering skills and interests. Knowing who has the needed skills for a particular project greatly helps in planning a community ministry.

Involvement

Depending on the nature of the project and the number of people needed, the next step is one of marketing and salesmanship. Be enthusiastic. Explain what will be done and why it needs to be done. Be specific in your request. Include all basic information such as the time of the project, place, date, and amount of time needed.

The more specific your appeal, the better. If you need a particular talent or skill, say so. Remember, people need to feel needed, and they need to be placed where they can succeed. A poor match will often result in frustration for everyone involved.

Some people like to learn new skills through volunteering. Some people even volunteer during periods of unemployment to retain skills, maintain a work record, learn new skills, and generally use their time more productively. Volunteerism by unemployed persons can even be the stepping-stone to employment when persons learn new skills, gain experience, and make contacts.

Never enlist people for a project by trying to make them feel guilty. They may end up participating but generally won't be happy and may resent you and the project. Be creative about how people can be involved. Some will want to participate but cannot attend. Are there other jobs they can do in preparation or follow-up?

Specific recruitment works best but some general publicity will be needed to acquaint the church with the project. If you need something built, appeal to the men's group (although do not overlook women who are handy with tools). If you want to work with children, talk to parents, teachers, or college students. If you need printed materials, seek out a person with a home computer and word processing skills.

Time is a valuable commodity. While some people never say no, others very sparingly say yes. Make your appeal for help specific in regard to duties and time commitment. Be sure people know why their help would make a difference.

A good time for involving others in ministry projects is in the fall right after school starts. Families generally build their schedules around two things: work and school. After the children have settled into their routines of ball practice and piano lessons, parents are more likely to be able to make time commitments. After the holidays is another good time to enlist people. The start of a new year often sparks interest in getting involved in something new.

Students generally have time during holiday breaks and summer. Plan projects to involve them that will occur during these times and recruit shortly beforehand.

Publicity

Utilize church resources to spread the word about community ministry.

•Place short articles and volunteer ads in your church newsletter.

•Make brief presentations in Sunday School classes, missions organizations, during announcements in worship services, and at other gatherings.

•Prepare a brochure or flier describing the project and the jobs which need to be done.

•Place posters or fliers on bulletin boards.

•Make personal contacts inviting people to take part in the ministry project.

•Have others tell about their experiences.

Scheduling

Be flexible in scheduling your group project. If your target group of participants is senior adults, schedule the event during the day, as many seniors do not like to be out at night. If you want to involve employed persons, try for an evening or weekend. Use people in behind-the-scenes work as well as the actual project.

Personal Satisfaction

Recognize that community ministry fulfills needs in our own lives even as we are serving others. We need to be mindful of this when we plan a ministry to involve others.

Some people need opportunities for personal interaction. Many need to feel appreciated and recognized. Others need to have opportunities to "do their thing"—paint, teach, sing, etc. Community ministry can be the means for fulfilling personal needs and yet reaching out to another person too!

To involve others in community ministry, you must first be sold on the idea yourself. You must believe in the cause. You must be committed to serving Christ through this ministry and believe the ministry is important.

Recognition

Recognize and thank each person who helps. If you are the project leader, take it upon yourself to express thanks to every individual who participates. A blanket thank you extended to the group is not nearly as effective. Personal notes and phone calls expressing appreciation will result in willing participants for the next ministry project.

Never ever treat people who volunteer like they owe you something. Volunteers help make your special project a success. Although you might think they should be doing this ministry "just because," the facts are that volunteers like to be appreciated.

Volunteers receive no monetary pay but they must be "paid." Although God rewards our unselfish service, he also uses those of us who are planners and organizers to meet needs in the lives of some of His children. Payment comes to volunteers through such things as a thank you, a personal note, a sense of self-fulfillment, a new skill learned, or just the satisfaction of helping another person.

Be God's channel for meeting the needs in your community *and* in the lives of those you enlist. A double blessing is in store.

Resources

Volunteerism

David E. Driver. *The Good Heart Book: A Guide to Volunteering.* Chicago: Noble Press, Inc., 1989.

Dass, Ram, and Paul Gorman. *How Can I Help?: Stories and Reflections on Service.* New York: Alfred A. Knopf, Inc., 1985.

Hollender, John A.. *How to Make the World a Better Place: A Beginner's Guide to Doing Good.* New York: William Morrow and Co., 1990.

O'Connell, Brian, and Ann Brown O'Connell. *Volunteers in Action.* New York: Foundation Center, 1989.

Collins, Gary R. *You Can Make a Difference: 14 Principles for Influencing Lives.* Grand Rapids: Zondervan Books, 1992.

Volunteer Management

Wilson, Marlene. *How to Mobilize Church Volunteers.* Minneapolis: Augsburg Publishing House, 1983.

Ellis, Susan J., and Katherine H. Noyes. *No Excuses: The Team Approach to Volunteer Management.* Philadelphia: Energize, Inc., 1981.

Morris, Margie. *Volunteer Ministries: New Strategies for Today's Church.* Available from Energize, Inc.

Silver, Nona. *At the Heart: The New Volunteer Challenge to Community Agencies.* San Francisco: San Francisco Foundation, 1988. Available from the National Volunteer Center.

For additional resources, write Energize, Inc., 5450 Wissahickon Avenue, Philadelphia, PA 19144 or phone 1 (800) 395-9800. A catalog of materials is available upon request.

Also contact the National Volunteer Center, 1111 North 19th Street, Suite 500, Arlington, VA 22209; (703) 276-0542. A complete catalog and sample newsletter are available upon request.

3

IDEAS FOR COMMUNITY MINISTRY

Probably the most difficult part of writing this material was attempting to categorize it. Most issues are multifaceted and interrelated with other issues. For instance, child abuse may be the result of alcoholism or homelessness the result of illiteracy and unemployment. Many times the apparent need is a symptom of other needs which must be met as well.

As you read through the ideas for community ministry, begin with prayer. We depend on the empowerment of God's Holy Spirit. Remember that missions is biblically based and includes both ministry and witness. Ask God to give you insight about witnessing through the particular avenue of service He would lead you to choose.

As you read this book and look for ministry ideas, read every section. Think about how issues of human need are interrelated. If you find an idea under one category that will work for you in another category, try it. The categories which follow are but an attempt to organize this book into something you can use. Unfortunately, space would not permit me to provide extensive details on how to carry out many of the ministry ideas. Rather, the purpose of this book is to get you thinking and point you in the right direction.

An index has been included at the back in order to cross-reference ideas and topics. There are often several terms used to refer to the same idea. For example, for *handicapped* you may also use *challenged* or *physically challenged*. For *retarded* you may also use *mentally challenged, developmentally challenged*, or *learning challenged*. Remember that terminology changes. Be aware of the new ways to refer to old problems and needs.

In particular, as a leader and concerned Christian, be sensitive to how others might be involved in ministry with you. Remember that different types of work appeal to different people. Look for many avenues of involvement.

Don't let the needs overwhelm you. Don't wait for others to get involved. Choose a need and get started. Others will join you in response to your testimony and enthusiasm.

Using This Book

Contact local groups. Ask for brochures about their work and use these to start a ministry information file. Even if you are not currently working in a particular area, background information may be helpful at some point in the future.

You may prefer to cut this book apart and put it

in a three-ring binder. As you find additional materials on particular areas of need or receive brochures from local groups, punch holes in these items and place them in the binder. By putting related materials together, you will have a ministry resource that can be expanded to include local resource materials and information as well as new items.

Selecting a Project

Because you will probably be squeezing community ministry into an already full schedule, choose something fun or meaningful to you. Although serious work, it can be enjoyable.

Talk with others about the project. If this is to be a group effort, be sure each person participates in the discussion. Also:
•Make a list of the volunteer work you and/or the group are doing now. Would members of the group be interested in helping with one of these projects?
•Make another list of things you have done before. Would you like to do any of these things?
•What areas of need interest you? What would you like to learn to do?

Look for projects that combine interests you already have with the opportunity to use your skills and/or learn new ones. Pray about the choice of a ministry project. God will reveal to you exactly what ministry would suit you best if you ask Him first, not after you've already made up your mind.

Resources

The Alban Institute, 4125 Nebraska Avenue, NW, Washington, DC 21106. 1 (800) 457-2674 (ordering); 1 (800) 242-5226 (consulting). A multidenominational membership organization dedicated to education, research, training, consulting and publishing materials for church ministry. Members receive a discount on publications, but you do not have to be a member to order.

A Church's Guide to Benevolent Ministries, Church Community Ministries, Florida Baptist Convention, 1230 Hendricks Avenue, Jacksonville, FL 32207. This notebook guide is available for $7.50.

"How to Begin" Series, Florida Baptist Convention, 1230 Hendricks Avenue, Jacksonville, FL 32207. Complete set available for $2.00 for out-of-state requests.

Titles include: "Clothes Closet"; "Food Pantry Ministry"; "Jail and Prison Ministries"; "A Tutoring Ministry"; "Mother's Morning Out"; "A Ministry with Latchkey Children"; "Big A Clubs"; "A Church Ministry to Alcoholics, Drug Abusers, Problem Drinkers and Their Families"; "A Ministry with the Homeless"; "Literacy Missions: Conversational English Ministry"; "Literacy Missions: Adult Reading and Writing."

"How-to" Booklets, Baptist General Convention of Texas, Church Ministries Department, 333 North Washington, Dallas, TX 75246-1798. Free to Texas Baptists, available to others for a nominal fee. A comprehensive packet (one of each title) is available for $15.00. Or booklets may be purchased separately. Write for a complete list and prices.

Home Mission Board, 1350 Spring Street, NW, Atlanta, GA 30367. Customer Service: 1 (800) 634-2642. *Church/Community Needs Survey Guide.*
"Hope for Hurting Humanity" Ministry Project Sheets.
The Home Mission Board (HMB) has a variety of free and priced ministry resource materials, many of which are referenced in this book. For an up-to-date listing and price information, order a *Home Mission Board Catalog.*

Baptist Book Stores carry many of the books cited as resources throughout this book. For the Baptist Book Store nearest you, contact the Customer Service Center at 1 (800) 458-2772; or for western states, 1 (800) 677-7797.

Woman's Missionary Union, P. O. Box 830010, Birmingham, AL 35283-0010. Customer Service: 1 (205) 991-4933.

Consumer's Resource Handbook, US Office of Consumer Affairs. Available free from the Consumer Information Center, Pueblo, CO 81009. Listings by state for a wide variety of services and agencies that could be resources in community ministry.

Local library—Your public library has many books, videos, and tapes on a variety of subjects. Don't overlook this valuable resource.

Bock, Betty. *You Can Make a Difference.* Birmingham, AL: Woman's Missionary Union, 1992.

Dudley, Carl S. *Basic Steps Toward Community Ministry.* Washington, DC: Alban Institute, 1991.

Crabtree, Davida F. *Empowering Church.* Washington DC: Alban Institute, 1989.

Stubblefield, Jerry. *Missions Activities for Men and Boys* Memphis: Brotherhood Commission, 1987.

Gainsburgh, Jonathan, and Jeanette Gainsburgh. *Christian Resource Directory.* Old Tappan, NJ: Fleming H. Revell Co. Directory gives over 20,000 listings of books, films, magazines, and ministries. Cross-referenced under 400 alphabetical titles.

ADDICTION MINISTRY

In *The Addictive Personality,* chemical-dependency specialist Craig Nakken calls the process of addiction the steady, predictable development of an unhealthy "relationship with an object or event." Home missionary Edwin Lilly says, "Understanding that Christianity does not eliminate addiction in the lives of individuals and/or families, or that it in any way makes them immune to such an affliction, is a must for anyone who wants to be of help in ministering to alcoholics and drug addicts and members of their families."

Substance abuse in the form of alcoholism, use of illegal drugs, and even dependence on prescription drugs affects every community. Drug use fosters many other problems. The issues of poverty, illiteracy, crime, abused children, etc., are often so interrelated that it is difficult to address one problem without the other.

Many substance abuse programs are indeed trying to help addicts in several areas of their lives. Volunteers are needed to help in a variety of ways.

Halfway Houses

Many halfway houses are operated by nonprofit local groups. They often do not receive much publicity because of the need to protect the very people they are trying to help. Contact your local volunteer action center or county office to learn about this type of work in your community.

Some halfway houses specifically minister to women and their children, recognizing that the children of addicted women suffer dire consequences as well. Other halfway houses deal with adults only. Often children are in foster care during this time.

Volunteers are needed in direct ministry with clients as well as in office/clerical support. Some needs are appropriate as group projects while others are best done as an individual or team. All halfway houses want to help the people they serve return to the community as fully functioning, self-supporting members of the community. Contact the halfway house in your area for additional information. Ask about these volunteer opportunities:

- Baby-sitters
- Clerk/Typist (type, file, stuff envelopes, etc.)
- Drivers (Medical appointments, job interviews, visit children, take to Alcoholics Anonymous or Narcotics Anonymous meetings)
- Maintenance (cleaning, carpenters, plumbers, electricians, painters)
- Pantry provider (pickups at local stores and churches, shopping)
- Recreation (art, music, aerobics, crafts)
- Spiritual counseling (Bible study, discussion groups, one-to-one)
- Surplus resources (sort clothing and other donations for usable items)
- Tutor/Teacher/Demonstrator:
    - Classroom, GED, or other tutoring
    - Cooking (one on one as well as organizing, preparing, and serving a meal for entire group)
    - Library skills
    - Personal living skills
    - Checkbook, savings accounts, budgeting
    - Shopping (price comparisons, planning ahead)
    - Nutrition
    - Health and beauty
    - Social skills, preparing for job interviews
    - Parenting skills

Support Groups

The self-help movement has grown dramatically. Groups patterned after the 12-step program of Alcoholics Anonymous can be found in every community for most any type of problem. Some groups are specifically Christian in their orientation and sponsorship. Others, while acknowledging a "higher power" and encouraging faith, do not go beyond this general term in order to include persons of all faith backgrounds.

Many churches allow various support groups to

meet in their buildings; or if you have identified a need for a support group, consider beginning this ministry in your church. Because of the anonymity factor, churches generally do not minister directly to the persons who attend Alcoholics Anonymous, Narcotics Anonymous, or other such groups. However, ministry opportunities with these groups exist.

Many of the persons who attend are single parents and cannot afford child care. Children must either sit in the meeting with their parents or go outside and play. Unsupervised children can pose problems. A weekly recreation time for the children of those who attend a support group would be a tremendous ministry to these families. Contact the group leader to inquire about this type of ministry.

Weekly child care to a support group is a very demanding ministry and would require a weekly commitment. Since not everyone can be there every week, this is a good project for a group, with a leader who will establish a staff rotation and lead in planning the weekly activities. This ministry will touch the lives of children and their parents.

Another avenue of ministry to support groups is providing refreshments for their meetings. Contact the group leader and express interest. Because of the anonymity factor and the fact that most groups do not promote any one church or faith, this will be an indirect ministry. However, most groups are willing to announce who provides the refreshments.

Ministry to the Family

All addictions affect the family as well as the abuser. Family members need emotional support as well as tangible help with related issues. Ministry to families could include:
- Counseling—group and individual
- Food
- Clothing
- Employment
- Emergency funds
- Referrals to community agencies and treatment programs

Prevention: The Best "Cure"

Substance abuse and alcoholism most commonly begin with experimentation and the desire to fit in a social scene. Regular use then leads to dependency, in which the user no longer gets a high, but needs the substance to feel normal. Ad-diction ministry must include education about the harmful effects of alcohol and drugs and must provide viable alternatives.

Rather than simply saying to children and youth, "Don't do it," we must give them information about what to do when confronted. We need to also provide alcohol- and drug-free alternative activities for those times when peer pressure is greatest—proms, school dances, football games, etc.

Do not hesitate to lead an educational campaign with youth. Enlist persons who are in recovery to talk with youth about the risks involved in choosing to drink or use drugs. Involve youth in planning seminars and workshops on alcohol and drug abuse. Encourage the formation of a SADD (Students Against Drunk Drivers) chapter.

Many parents and concerned community leaders are forming neighborhood councils or support groups to fight alcohol and drug abuse among kids. By joining together, they can take steps to reinforce the guidance from home. The groups discuss concerns and support and advise one another. Group members network to be sure that neighborhood kids are taking part in safe activities and eliminating the excuse "everyone else is doing it." Starting this type of group is not a typical Baptist Women project. But this project has a tremendous impact on the community.

Granny House

Many mothers refuse to enter addiction treatment programs for fear they will lose their children. Although the goal of foster care is to reunite families whenever possible, it does not always work. Granny House is a concept that was developed in an Atlanta public housing project. Children of addicted mothers are cared for in an apartment within the complex by community residents trained as on-site foster parents. The children's regular routines are maintained as closely as possible while the mothers are in treatment. For more information about Granny House, contact the Atlanta Housing Authority, 739 West Peachtree Street, NW, Atlanta, GA 30365; (404) 892-4700.

An alternative idea on a smaller scale is to be available to care for children in your community while parents are in detoxification and rehabilitation programs. If parents can make arrangements for the care of children and enter a program voluntarily, it is better for the children and the parents.

Where to Get Additional Help

•Public agencies: Health Department, Department of Social Services.
•Local chapters of these organizations: Alcoholics Anonymous, Narcotics Anonymous, Al-Anon, Alateen, Nar-Anon, Cocaine Anonymous, Salvation Army, Mothers Against Drunk Driving (MADD).
•State convention and associational church and community ministries directors

Resources

Alcohol and drug abuse prevention resources are available from the Christian Life Commission, 901 Commerce Street, Suite 550, Nashville, TN 37203-3620. (615) 244-2495.

Home Mission Board: "Beginning a Ministry with Substance Abusers" (366-18F); "Substance Abusers" (365-32F); "How to Begin a Ministry with Substance Abusers" (365-36F).

Baptist Sunday School Board Equipping Center Module: *Dealing with Addiction.* Six-session study for adults teaching facts about addiction and how to minister.

Baptist General Convention of Texas, Christian Life Commission, 333 North Washington Street, Dallas, TX 75246-1798; (214) 828-5100. ON TRAC is a drug abuse prevention program developed by BGCT. Contact them for a brochure which describes the program in detail and gives the price information.

National Council on Alcoholism and Drug Dependence, Inc. (NCADD), 12 West 21st Street, New York, NY 10010; 1 (800) NCA-CALL. National nonprofit organization combating alcoholism, drug addiction, and related problems. Ask for their brochure "Talking With Your Child About Alcohol: A Step By Step Guide for Parents and Other Caring Grown-ups."

Alcoholics Anonymous, P. O. Box 459, Grand Central Station, New York, NY 10163; (212) 686-1100.

American Council for Drug Education, 204 Monroe Street, Rockville, MD 20850; 1 (800) 488-DRUG. Independent, nonprofit membership organization committed to drug education.

National Clearinghouse for Alcohol and Drug Information (NCADI), P. O. Box 2345, Rockville, MD 20852; (301) 468-2600.

Hazelden Educational Materials, P. O. Box 176, Center City, MN 55012-0176; 1 (800) 328-9000. Assorted books for children and families where there is chemical dependency. Titles include: *I Can Talk About What Hurts, My House Is Different,* and *The Brown Bottle.* Call for a free catalog.

Serendipity, P. O. Box 1012, Littleton, CO 80160. 1 (800) 525-9563. Order a catalog of resources for support groups and other small group Bible studies. The support group series includes:
  •*12-Steps for Christians: The Path to Wholeness*
  •*Addictive Lifestyles: Breaking Free*
  •*Adult Children of Alcoholics*
  •*Co-Dependency: Learning to Say "Enough"*
  •*Divorce Recovery: Picking Up the Pieces*

Growing Up Drug Free: A Parent's Guide to Prevention. Call the United States Department of Education, 1 (800) 624-0100, to obtain a free copy.

Williams, David J. *Parenting for Prevention.* Minneapolis: Johnson Institute Books, 1988.

Alcohol: A Christian Student's Response. Nashville: Convention Press, 1992.

Dickson, Charles. *Beating the Chemical Cop-out.* Birmingham, AL: World Changers Resources, 1992.

Dockrey. Karen. *Alone But Not Lonely.* Birmingham, AL: World Changers Resources, 1993.

Dockrey, Karen. *Curing the Self-hate Virus.* Birmingham, AL: World Changers Resources, 1993.

Martin, Sara Hines. *Meeting Needs Through Support Groups.* Birmingham, AL: New Hope, 1992.

AIDS MINISTRY

In response to the AIDS epidemic, there is a growing number of community groups and organizations that have been specifically formed to help AIDS victims and their families. Because this is a progressive disease, the particular help needed will depend upon the stage of the disease. But throughout their illness, AIDS patients need support and friendship.

AIDS patients may need the services of other programs for related problems such as substance abuse. Community groups that work with AIDS patients will refer to other groups when necessary. However, the main focus of AIDS support groups and ministries is to work directly with the AIDS patient and provide assistance as needed.

To learn about Christian AIDS ministries in your area, contact the Christian AIDS Service Alliance, 3 Church Circle, #108, Annapolis, MD 21401. Or you may call them at (301) 268-3442.

Contact your local health department to find out what is being done locally to provide services to persons with AIDS. The National AIDS Information Clearinghouse (1 [800] 458-5231) and the National AIDS Hotline (1 [800] 342-AIDS, tape; or 1 (800) 342-7514, operator) both provide general information, types of services, and information about local services.

Buddy System

Volunteers provide services that range from driving an AIDS patient to the grocery store or filling prescriptions to assisting with housekeeping chores. This is a ministry of friendship that can be much like any other ministry to terminally ill persons. A person with AIDS often tires easily, so help with even simple tasks is appreciated. However, do not do what the person wants to do for himself. Always ask.

One of the frequent needs is transportation. AIDS is a progressive disease and the patient gets weaker and weaker, making driving difficult. Medications also can make the AIDS victims so sick, that they cannot drive. Frequent trips to the doctor and to the hospital make this a real need and ministry opportunity.

Witnessing

Share your faith but don't be overbearing. The question Do you know Jesus personally? or Are you in the process of discovering Who He is? can be an entry point for sharing the gospel. Sometimes the best witness is praying with the person and continuing to show kindness.

Support Groups

Provide support for AIDS patients, caregivers, parents and friends, for people who are HIV-positive. Offer to go with the AIDS patient or family member. Many are nervous about going to such a meeting the first time.

Children with AIDS

A growing number of children are being born with AIDS. Their life expectancy is short. Persons who can volunteer to help with their care are desperately needed.

Holiday Baskets and Flowers

Tangible expressions of concern are always welcome. One local AIDS ministry group involves people in making and delivering baskets and/or flowers at the holidays to AIDS patients. These are seasonally decorated and contain holiday food items, cards, and Scripture portions. This is a project that can involve adults, youth, and children.

Education

Most people suffer from ICHTM—the "It Can't Happen to Me" syndrome. Teenagers in particular need Christian sex education that teaches them how AIDS is spread and the biblical basis for abstinence from sexual activity until marriage. While this is a social/moral issue, more churches need to include this type of education in community ministry programs.

Where to Get Additional Help

•Public agencies: Health Department, Department of Social Services
•National AIDS Clearinghouse, P. O. Box 6003, Rockville, MD 20850. 1 (800) 458-5231. Brochures, displays, free and priced materials for AIDS education.
•State convention and associational church and community ministries directors

Resources

Baptist Center for Ethics: *What Parents with Children K–12 Should Know About AIDS; Babies with AIDS: The Church's Calling*

Home Mission Board: "Beginning a Ministry with People with AIDS" (632-76F)

Anderson, Monnie. *Ideas for Hospital Ministries.* Birmingham: New Hope, 1992. Chapter 10, "AIDS: A New Challenge for the Church," gives an excellent overview of what AIDS is , how it is transmitted, and beginning AIDS ministries.

Bartlett, John G., MD, and Ann K. Finkbeiner. *The Guide to Living with HIV Infection.* Baltimore: Johns Hopkins University Press, 1991.

Tillman, William M., Jr. *AIDS: A Christian Response.* Nashville: Convention Press, 1990.

Payne, Franklin E. *What Every Christian Should Know About the AIDS Epidemic: The Medical and Biblical Facts About AIDS.* Augusta: Covenant Books, 1992.

Amos, William E., Jr. *When AIDS Comes to Church.* Philadelphia: Westminster Press, 1988.

Cummings, Margaret Ann. *Touched by AIDS.* Birmingham, AL: World Changers Resources, 1992.

Bock, Betty. *You Can Make a Difference.* Birmingham, AL: Woman's Missionary Union, 1992.

Martin, Sara Hines. *Meeting Needs Through Support Groups.* Birmingham, AL: New Hope, 1992.

BAPTIST CENTERS AND CHURCH WEEKDAY MINISTRIES

Southern Baptists have attempted to combine a variety of ministries in needy areas through Baptist Centers. Generally found in the inner city, Baptist centers combine social ministries with a Christian witness. They are reaching people who would not otherwise attend a church. Although not always called Baptist centers, church and community weekday ministries provided by inner-city churches have the same type of focus and need for volunteers.

Partnership

A meaningful way to establish an ongoing relationship with a Baptist center or inner-city church is through two-way partnerships of suburban and inner-city congregations. Such partnerships would not be primarily financial, although certainly some Baptist centers or inner-city churches could benefit from such support. Rather, partnership would link individuals and organizations together, such as women's groups, Sunday School classes, or youth groups. Through dialogue, visits, and sharing of concerns, each congregation can learn from one another.

Volunteers

Baptist centers generally have a director or pastor/director who administers the overall work of the center. Consistent volunteers are needed to assist in every area of work done by the Baptist center or inner city congregation. Even if a volunteer only does one thing, if done on a consistent basis, this multiplies the effectiveness of the director and frees this person to do other tasks.

Christian Social Ministries

Because of the familiar litany of abuse, poverty, alcoholism, drug addiction, and broken homes that plague our cities, Baptist centers provide a variety of services and ministries. To provide some of these ministries, groups and individuals are needed to collect, sort, and distribute various items. Volunteers are desperately needed to work directly with people in need, distributing items that have been provided by others and sharing the gospel of Christ in the ministry context.

Ministries which are provided by Baptist centers include:
- Emergency food pantry.
- Clothes closet.
- Senior adult meal program—Hot meal, fellowship.
- Children's clubs.
- Youth programs.
- Super pantry—A self-help program in basic life skills.
- Aerobics classes.
- Mother's club—Guest speakers, fellowship, singing, prayer, refreshments.
- Counseling—Individual and group.

- Support groups.
- Child care—Provides employment for community residents as well as affordable day care for low income families.
- Afterschool programs—Latchkey, Big A Clubs, recreation, sports, crafts.
- Health clinics—Provide basic health care for working poor on a "pay what you can afford" basis. Doctors, nurses, and other volunteers provide preventive medical care, treat minor illnesses, and teach health education.
- Tutoring, GED classes.
- Arts and crafts, sewing, cooking classes for adults.
- Power hour—Youth discipleship classes.
- Summer day camp.
- Vacation Bible School.
- Worship.
- Bible study.
- Music—Choirs and other music programs.

Contact the director to learn about items which you can collect for the Baptist center. Ask about the on-going need for volunteers and how you might help with a regular program or activity. If your group would prefer to do a one-time project, inquire about a specific need you might fill.

Church Weekday Ministries and Benevolence Ministries

Many churches have weekday ministries similar to those provided by Baptist centers. Many of the ministries in this book would come under the title church and community ministries.

Where to Get Additional Help

- State Baptist convention office: Current director's name and address of a Baptist center in your area; assistance with starting church and community ministries in your community.
- State convention and associational church and community ministries directors

Resources

Home Mission Board: "Beginning Church Weekday Ministries" (366-23F); "Weekday Ministries: Church and Community Missions" (366-01F).

Florida Baptist Convention: *How to Begin a Clothes Closet; A Church's Guide to Benevolent Ministries.*

Baptist General Convention of Texas: *How to Begin Weekday Ministries in a Smaller Membership Church; Weekday Mission Ministries Provided by Local Churches; How to Begin the Church Community Club Program.*

BAPTIST CENTERS/OTHER MINISTRY POINTS

Alabama
RUSSELL ASSOCIATION CENTER
P. O. Box 966
Phenix City, AL 36898-0966
(205) 298-3581

BAPTIST CENTER
2501 12th Avenue, North
Birmingham, AL 35234-3114
(205) 591-1927

BAPTIST CENTER
1200 South Hull Street
Montgomery, AL 36104
(205) 263-3271

Arizona
SHARING MINISTRIES
INNER-CITY BOARDER MINISTRY SITE
P. O. Box 50381
Tucson, AZ 85703-1381
(602) 623-9023

RIO VISTA BAPTIST CENTER
1431 East Southern Avenue
Phoenix, AZ 85040

Arkansas
MIGRANT MISSION CENTER
Route 4, Box 1889
Hope, AR 71801
(501) 777-8219

BARTHOLOMEW MIGRANT MISSION CENTER
P. O. Box 983
Warren, AR 71671-0983
(501) 463-8480

California
BAPTIST MINISTRIES CENTER
4212 Clara Street
Cudahy, CA 90201

TELEGRAPH BAPTIST CENTER
5316 Telegraph Avenue
Oakland, CA 94609
(415) 658-4457

COMMUNITY BAPTIST CENTER
111 Orange Avenue
Coronado, CA 92118-1408
(619) 435-8121

District of Columbia
JOHENNING BAPTIST CENTER
4025 Ninth Street, SE
Washington, DC 20032-6051
(202) 561-5200

Florida
THE BAPTIST CENTER
123 Kraft Avenue
Panama City, FL 32401
(904) 763-8892

MOBILE DENTAL CLINIC
Route 8, Box 479
Lake City, FL 32055
(904) 755-7827

Georgia
FLOYD ASSOCIATION CENTER
300 Chatillon Road, NE
Rome, GA 30161-4911
(404) 291-0904

SAVANNAH BAPTIST CENTER
313 East Harris Street
Savannah, GA 31401-4617
(912) 232-1033

MEMORIAL DRIVE CENTER
560 Memorial Dr., SE
Atlanta, GA 30317-1802
(404) 378-2990

CLARK HOWELL–TECHWOOD
BAPTIST CENTER
156 Parker Street, NW
Atlanta, GA 30313-2140
(404) 881-1291

STEWART BAPTIST CENTER
P. O. Box 17772
Atlanta, GA 30316
(404) 522-0942

UNITED BAPTIST CENTER
1332 Stewart Avenue
Atlanta, GA 30310
(404) 758-2602

Illinois
EAST ST. LOUIS CENTER
540 North 6th Street
East St. Louis, IL 62201-1320
(618) 847-5615

UPTOWN BAPTIST CHURCH
1011 West Wilson
Chicago, IL 60640
(312) 784-2922

Indiana
METROPOLITAN BAPTIST
CENTER
952 North Pennsylvania
Indianapolis, IN 46204-1032
(317) 687-0075

Iowa
FRIENDSHIP BAPTIST CENTER
P. O. Box 2455
Des Moines, IA 50311
(515) 244-1701

Kansas
GOOD NEIGHBOR BAPTIST
CENTER
1157 North Emporia
Wichita, KS 67214-2806
(316) 264-1061

WYANDOTTE BAPTIST CENTER
Kansas City, KS 66062
(913) 299-0294

Kentucky
BAPTIST FELLOWSHIP CENTER
1351 Catalpa Street
Louisville, KY 40211-1730
(502) 774-2734

JEFFERSON STREET BAPTIST
CENTER
753 East Jefferson Street
Louisville, KY 40202
(502) 584-6543

FREEDA HARRIS BAPTIST
CENTER
Box 190
Lookout, KY 41542-0190
(606) 754-7414

WHEELWRIGHT BAPTIST
CENTER
Box 73
Wheelwright, KY 41669-0073
(606) 452-2051

Louisiana
ABRAHAM MISSION
2455 Highway 28 East
Pineville, LA 71360
(318) 445-8384

RIGHT CHOICE TEEN CENTER
220 West Main Street
New Iberia, LA 70560
(318) 364-8128

LASALLE STOREFRONT
MINISTRY
HC60, Box 754
Jena, LA 71342
(318) 992-6272

BAPTIST MISSION CENTER
221 Beaubouef Road
Deville, LA 71320
(318) 466-3158

CITY PRICE BAPTIST MISSION
P. O. Box 282
Port Sulphur, LA 70083
(504) 564-3817

BRANTLEY BAPTIST CENTER
201 Magazine Street
New Orleans, LA 70130
(504) 523-5761

CARVER BAPTIST CENTER
3701 Annunciation
New Orleans, LA 70115-5397
(504) 897-2434

RACHEL SIMS MISSION CENTER
729 Second Street
New Orleans, LA 70130-5439
(504) 891-2578

BAPTIST FRIENDSHIP HOUSE
813 Elysian Fields Avenue
New Orleans, LA 70117
(504) 949-4469

STOREFRONT MINISTRY CENTER
2596 Clear Lake Road
Pioneer, LA 71266
(318) 428-2762

LINWOOD MISSION CENTER
1622 Midway
Shreveport, LA 71108
(318) 631-4467

HOLY GHOST BAPTIST STORE-
FRONT MINISTRY
P. O. Box 82802
Baton Rouge, LA 70884-2802
(504) 383-1333

GRACE FELLOWSHIP MINISTRY
CENTER
1345 Gardere Lane
Baton Rouge, LA 70820
(504) 766-3260

CORNERSTONE BAPTIST
MISSION
104-A Bayou Pacquet
Slidell, LA 70122
(504) 282-9728

BEAUREGARD MISSION CENTER
Route 2, Box 1120
Colfax, LA 71417
(504) 627-5138

FERRIDAY STOREFRONT MIS-
SION
P. O. Box 188
Clayton, LA 71326
(504) 717-3267

BREADCRUMB BAPTIST MINISTRY
CENTER
108 Temple Street
Jonesville, LA 71343
(318) 339-8713

Maryland
CANTON BAPTIST CENTER
3302 Toone Street
Baltimore, MD 212245118
(301) 563-1177

KATHLEEN MALLORY CENTER
1127 Riverside Avenue
Baltimore, MD 21230
(410) 539-1406

SEVENTH BAPTIST MINISTRY
24 East North Avenue
Baltimore, MD 21202
(410) 837-3797

Michigan
THE BAPTIST CENTER
2700 2nd Avenue
Detroit, MI 48201
(313) 961-9075

Missouri
GRAND OAK MISSION CENTER
2854 West Grand
Springfield, MO 65802
(417) 869-4818

BAPTIST CENTER
5301 Sheridan Drive
Jefferson City, MO 65109

BLUE RIVER/KANSAS CITY
CENTER
4001 NE Lakewood Way
Lees Summit, MO 64064
(816) 795-1822

Nebraska
OMAHA BAPTIST CENTER
1030 S. 24th Street
Omaha, NE 68108-3022
(402) 346-6667

New Mexico
BAPTIST NEIGHBORHOOD
CENTER
1020 Edith Boulevard, SE
Albuquerque, NM 87102
(505) 247-2552

New York
GRAFFITI BAPTIST CENTER
184 East 7th Street
New York, NY 10009
(212) 473-0044

WAKE EDEN COMMUNITY
MINISTRY
2026 Strang Avenue
Bronx, NY 10466
(212) 325-8056

North Carolina
GASTON BAPTIST CENTER
1607 Ranklin Lake Road
Gastonia, NC 27565
(704) 867-7257

WELCOME INN BAPTIST CENTER
2734 Commerce Road
Jacksonville, NC 28540
(919) 347-3146

Ohio
STOWE MEMORIAL CENTER
P. O. Box 06341
Columbus, OH 43206
(614) 443-1120

BAPTIST CENTER
127 Mulberry Street
Cincinnati, OH 45210-1124
(513) 241-0283

NEW LIFE BAPTIST MISSION
CENTER
402 Hudson Avenue
Hamilton, OH 45011
(513) 894-9515

CENTRAL BAPTIST MISSION
CENTER
919 Johnston Street
Akron, OH 44306
216/762-3786

EDGEWOOD BAPTIST MISSION
CENTER
P. O. Box 7326
Dayton, OH 45407-0326
(513) 223-1383

Oklahoma
BAPTIST MISSION CENTER
2125 Exchange Avenue
Oklahoma City, OK 73108
(405) 235-6162

BAPTIST EDUCATIONAL CENTER
1405 North Cincinnati
Tulsa, OK 74106
(918) 582-7731

BAPTIST WOMEN'S SHELTER
658 North Boulder
Tulsa, OK 74106
(918) 584-2666

GRACE RESCUE MISSION
2205 Exchange Avenue
Oklahoma City, OK 73108
(405) 232-5756

Oregon
BAPTIST REVIVAL CENTER
2050 Northwest Everett
Portland, OR 97209-1011
(503) 243-2714

Rhode Island
SMITH HILL BAPTIST MINISTRY
102 Oakland Avenue
Providence, RI 02908
(401) 861-1863

Tennessee
WESTERN HEIGHTS BAPTIST
CENTER
1230 West Scott Avenue
Knoxville, TN 37921-6682
(615) 525-9068

MONTGOMERY BAPTIST CENTER
4601 Joe Lewis Road
Knoxville, TN 37920
(615) 577-6244

MILITARY OASIS
5281 Navy Road
Millington, TN 38053-2535
901/872-1144

BLYTHE AVENUE BAPTIST
CENTER
P. O. Box 3477
Cleveland, TN 37320-3477
(615) 478-1777

HOLSTON ASSOCIATION
CENTER
207 University Parkway
Johnson City, TN 37604
(615) 929-1196

Texas
GANO BAPTIST CENTER
1815 Gano
Houston, TX 77009
(713) 227-0304

BAPTIST MISSION CENTER
1913 Fletcher
Houston, TX 77009
(713) 227-6371

JOY FELLOWSHIP CENTER
7629 Avenue F
Houston, TX 77012
(713) 921-0197

COMMUNITY BAPTIST CENTER
2000 East Second Street
Austin, TX 78702
(512) 472-7592

BAPTIST COMMUNITY CENTER
915 East Peach Street
Fort Worth, TX 76102
(817) 336-1922

CRISIS PREGNANCY CENTER
4520 James Avenue
Fort Worth, TX 76115-2117
(817) 560-2226

CLIFF TEMPLE BAPTIST CENTER
P. O. Box 3770
Dallas, TX 75208
(214) 942-6407

CALVARY HOUSE
2710 I-H-10 East
Beaumont, TX 77703
(409) 898-8797

Utah
BAPTIST CONCERN CENTER
1235 West California Avenue
Salt Lake City, UT 84102
(801) 972-5708

Vermont
RESURRECTION BAPTIST
CENTER
144 Elm Street
Montpelier, VT 05602
(802) 223-6538

Virginia
SOUTH RICHMOND BAPTIST
CENTER
1101 Bainbridge Street
Richmond, VA 23224
(804) 232-0174

OREGON HILL BAPTIST CENTER
400 South Pine Street
Richmond, VA 23220
(804) 648-1353

HILLSIDE BAPTIST CENTER
1708 Harwood Street
Richmond, VA 23224
(804) 233-5661

CHURCH HILL MINISTRY
CENTER
2800 P Street
Richmond, VA 23223
(804) 780-0053

BLAND MINISTRY CENTER
Box 211
Bland, VA 24315
(703) 688-4701

BAPTIST COMMUNITY CENTER
101 17th Street, SE
Roanoke, VA 24013
(703) 342-8452

FRIENDSHIP HOUSE
635 Elm Avenue, SW
Roanoke, VA 24016
(703) 343-5437

DOWNTOWN MINISTRY CENTER
345 McClean Street
Portsmouth, VA 23701
(804) 487-3918

FRIENDSHIP HOUSE
40 King's Way
Hampton, VA 23606
(804) 728-9420

BAPTIST CENTER
835 Bolling Avenue
Charlottesville, VA 22901
(804) 977-4375

BEREAVEMENT CARE MINISTRY

Grief over the loss of a loved one is universal. The need for ministry to grieving persons has grown in an age when we no longer live in close-knit family units and have the support of the family at such times. This type of ministry spans the church and community, as often the church is called upon to be a resource to families who have little or no connection with the church.

Consider forming a bereavement care team. This would be a team of persons who are trained by a pastor, counselor, or hospital chaplain in grief ministry. They would be available to support the work of the pastor in ministry to bereaved persons, in and out of the church. Contact your local hospice program or counseling service for information about such training.

At the time of the loss, any or all of the following actions may be appropriate:
- Visit the family.
- Prepare food.
- Offer to stay with children, elderly adults, or any family member who might need care.
- Help with housework or yard work to help prepare for guests.

After the loss, continue to minister to the person/family:
- Write a note a week or two later. Acknowledge that you understand that grief is a healing process that occurs slowly over time. Indicate that you are available. Inform the grieving person of services that are available such as a bereavement program or support group. Indicate that you will call soon to see how they are doing.
- Make a home visit (or phone call, if necessary) three to four weeks after the loss. Informally, do a bereavement assessment (see checklist following).
- Find out birthdates (theirs and the deceased) and anniversaries. Send notes or cards at these times. Make contact during the holidays and remember the anniversary of the death. These are rough times for a grieving person.
- Be a grief companion. Don't give advice, rather be there to listen, lend support. Grieving persons often need to retell the story many times.

Bereavement Assessment

In follow-up visits or calls, look for signs that a person is not working through grief. Some simple questions can help you know if the person needs additional support. Ask questions and listen to what the person says as well as what they don't say. Ask questions like these:
- Have your sleeping or eating patterns changed?
- What kind of support system do you have? Family?
- Is the family supportive and helpful?
- Is there someone you can really talk to when you're feeling down?
- Are you back to work, volunteering, family gatherings, or recreational pursuits?
- Has your financial status changed?
- Have you seen a doctor lately?

If there has been a change in residence, be especially sensitive to extended grief. The person is not only grieving the loss of a loved one, but also for the place they lived and their way of life. Be on the lookout for signs of alcohol or drug abuse.

If the loss has been the death of a child, be aware that the divorce rate is about 90 percent. Men and women grieve differently. Help couples talk to each other about their grief in order to preserve the marriage.

Recognize various circumstances that will affect grief such as a dysfunctional family or the particular circumstances of the death or loss. Suicide or murder invoke far more anger or guilt than the peaceful death of an elderly person.

A good bereavement team member is one who has gone through the process of loss and recovery. A *limited* amount of self-disclosure is useful. However, do not tell the grieving person that you know how they feel, because you don't. Too much disclosure can backfire by turning the attention to you rather than the grieving person. Be calm and compassionate. A good bereavement volunteer is also a good listener.

Bereavement Support Group

Consider forming a bereavement support group. This is not just a place for people to tell their story. It needs to include education about how to go on living. It should be a safe place for people to express their emotions of grief and receive encouragement and new ideas.

Bereavement support groups may explore these topics: anger, guilt, wellness and holistic health, spiritual growth, financial planning, safety tips, living and traveling alone, cooking for one, assertiveness training, children and loss, spousal loss, the loss of a child, donating your body to science, organ donation.

People grieve over many things. The grief process over the loss of a job, breakup of a marriage, unexpected move, or other traumatic change can be just as intense as grief at the loss of a loved one. Taking the initiative to befriend a person who is grieving is an important community ministry that can be done by individuals or groups.

Where to Get Additional Help

•Public agencies
•Hospital Hospice Programs
•Local chapters of Mental Health Association and Compassionate Friends
•Hospital chaplain

•Baptist General Convention of Texas: "Ministry to Widowed Persons."

•The Compassionate Friends, P. O. Box 3696, Oak Brook, IL 60522-3696. (312) 323-5010. This nationwide support group for bereaved parents and siblings produces a series of brochures and other materials. Titles include:
When a Child Dies
Understanding Grief
Stillbirth, Miscarriage, and Infant Death
Suggestions for Medical Personnel
Caring for Surviving Children
Surviving Your Child's Suicide
Suggestions for Clergy
Suggestions for Teachers and School Counselors
When an Employee is Grieving
When a Brother or Sister Dies
How Can I Help
When a Co-worker is Grieving
First Responders
Understanding Grief . . . When a Grandchild Dies

•Serendipity, P. O. Box 1012, Littleton, CO 80160; 1 (800) 525-9563. Support group/Bible study: *Dealing with Grief and Loss*.

Resources

James, John W., and Frank Cherry. *The Grief Recovery Handbook: A Step by Step Program for Moving Beyond Loss*. New York: Harper and Row, 1988.

Branch, Roger, and Larry A. Platt. *Resources for Ministry in Death and Dying*. Nashville: Broadman Press, 1988.

Kolf, June. *Teenagers Talk About Grief*. Grand Rapids: Baker Book House, 1990.

Mumford, Amy Ross. *It Hurts to Lose a Special Person*. Denver: Accent Books, 1982.

Claypool, John. *Tracks of a Fellow Struggler*. Waco: Word Inc., 1982.

Dyson, Ernest. *Living with God in Loss*. Nashville: Broadman Press, 1989.

Stevens, Velma D. *Grief Work*. Nashville: Broadman Press, 1990.

Grollman, Earl A. *Talking About Death: A Dialogue Between Parent and Child*. Boston: Beacon Press, 1991.

Swain, Claudia Jones. *Looking at Loss* (My Experience with Miscarriage). Birmingham, AL: New Hope, 1988.

Yarbrough, Lynn. *Spring Follows Winter* (My Experience with the Death of My Husband). Birmingham, AL: New Hope, 1987.

Martin, Sara Hines. *Meeting Needs Through Support Groups.* Birmingham, AL: New Hope, 1992.

Dockrey, Karen. *It's Not Fair!* Birmingham, AL: World Changers Resources, 1992.

CHILDREN AND YOUTH

Children in all locations, urban, suburban, and rural, need special attention. Many nonprofit groups and community agencies work to help children of all economic and social backgrounds. Volunteers are needed for on-going work as well as one-time or seasonal projects.

Back to School

Provide new school supplies for children in the community. Bags containing new pencils, notebooks, crayons, and a bookmark encourage children and parents who are struggling financially. Include Scripture portions designed for children.

Social Services

Contact your local Department of Social Services about a waiting room ministry. Parents applying for assistance need help with small children while they are completing applications.

Transportation for social services clients can be a tremendous individual or team ministry. This would include transportation for clients who might otherwise miss clinic and other important appointments or transportation for children to and from day care. The opportunity for interaction between the volunteer and the client can play an important role in the rehabilitative process. For instance, demonstrating patience with a mother who is having difficulty getting a child ready on time can have a profound effect on the parent. A good relationship with the child reassures the child and provides a positive relationship with another adult.

Mentoring

Big Brothers/Big Sisters and other programs that match an adult with a youngster are always in need of volunteers. One-to-one work involves being a friend and including the youngster in your family interests and activities. A family can undertake this ministry as well. Positive relationships with adults can reduce dropouts, teen pregnancies, substance abuse, and delinquency.

Hospitals and Other Facilities

Volunteers are needed to provide physical contact and "cuddling" to hospitalized abused or neglected children. Babies of addicted mothers need lots of care, more than the hospital staff can provide. Volunteers rock and stroke babies to provide that much-needed loving human contact.

Reading Clubs

Sponsor a summer or afterschool reading club for children. The club can be held in your church library, a home, recreation center, or multipurpose room in an apartment complex. Bring children's books and encourage reading. Plan thematic programs and bring books that develop the theme.

Also, provide children's books that deal with children's concerns such as divorce, alcoholic parents, and fighting parents. As appropriate, read these with children to allow them an opportunity to talk about their feelings through discussing the book.

Tutoring

Volunteers are needed in the schools to work with children one-to-one and in small groups. You do not have to have a child enrolled in a local school to volunteer.

Consider making your home a "Homework House." Invite neighborhood children to stop by on certain days of the week, at set hours, for help with homework. This could also be done as an afterschool ministry at the church or community recreation center one or more days a week.

Or volunteer to help with an existing tutoring program in your community. Many opportunities for building relationships with the child and the family will develop.

Big A Clubs

Start a Bible club for unchurched children in your community. This could meet in a home, recreation center, apartment complex, or park. Big A Clubs are designed to meet once a week for one hour. Materials are easy to use and are a flexible resource for any setting. The Teacher's Book, Resource Kit, and Pupils' Take-Home pieces are available.

Latchkey Ministry

Latchkey is a form of afterschool day care for school-age children, generally from kindergarten through grade 5. Many communities offer latchkey programs that operate right in the school building or in a recreation center. Parents generally pay for the service just as they would day care for younger children.

Because this is a form of day care, state guidelines for its operation must be followed. This includes licensing, zoning, and compliance with health and fire regulations. Determine the need and research local requirements for starting this type of ministry.

Many existing programs would welcome volunteers. However, because of state and local licensing regulations, volunteers may have to be fingerprinted and have a police background check before being allowed to help. This is standard procedure in many child care settings.

Child Abuse

Child abuse takes many, often multiple, forms: verbal, emotional, sexual. Do not hesitate to get involved. If a child in your church, neighborhood, or school shows signs of physical abuse, report it. Listen carefully to what children say in settings where they are comfortable with the adult leaders.

Recreation

Many communities have recreation and sports programs for children that are completely staffed by volunteers. Although these are non-sectarian programs, many opportunities for building relationships with children and their families arise from these community recreation programs. Often the number of children who can participate is limited by the number of adult volunteers and coaches.

This is a good ministry for an individual or a group. A women's group, for example, could offer to teach a particular class each week at a local recreation center. This would provide continuity of leadership even when someone had to miss a week. Look for the opportunities to minister to the extended family as well. Do not hesitate to offer a Christian witness when a parent thanks you for taking time to work with his or her child.

Send a Child to Camp

Summer camp can be a great time of learning and a positive change of environment for a youngster. However, the expense is often beyond the means of many families. Contact your church, association, or local children's program about helping with camp expenses.

If possible, take the child to camp. Volunteer to serve as a camp counselor, cook, recreation leader, or other helper. Older youth can often assist in children's camp programs as well.

Day camping programs as well as residential camp programs need volunteers.

YouthBuild Program and Coalition

Around the nation communities are establishing programs to help youth who have dropped out of school. YouthBuild is a model of youth employment and training in construction and rehabilitation of housing for homeless and low-income people. It was first implemented in East Harlem by the Youth Action Program and has been successfully replicated in other communities.

Students who participate spend half their time in academic studies, and half in construction training. The federal government has included funds for YouthBuild as a part of the drive for national affordable housing. Coalition members write and call legislators to encourage funding of this program. In addition, interested school districts, churches, and other organizations can learn how to establish a YouthBuild program in the community. Planning Resources, Implementation Manual, Construction Training Curriculum, and other materials are available from YouthBuild. Contact YouthBuild USA, 366 Marsh Street, Belmont, MA 02178; (617) 489-3400.

Where to Get Additional Help

•Public agencies: Department of Social Services, local schools, school boards, Recreation Department
•State convention and associational church and community ministries directors

Resources

Florida Baptist Convention: "How to Begin a Tutoring Ministry," "How to Begin Big A Clubs," "How to Begin a Ministry with Latchkey Children."

Home Mission Board: "How to Begin a Church Weekday Ministry" (366-13F); "Beginning Church Weekday Ministries" (366-23F).

Woman's Missionary Union: "Do You Dream of Doing Something That Will Change the World?" (Available from state WMU offices.)

Baptist General Convention of Texas: "Weekday Mission Ministries Provided by Local Churches," "Weekday Ministries in a Smaller Membership Church," "How to Begin Weekday Child Care Ministry," "Mother's Day Out Program," "How to Begin a Church Community Tutoring Program."

Big A Club materials: Teacher's Book, Resource Kit, Pupils' Take-Home Pieces for Unit 1 and Unit 2, English or Spanish. Available through Baptist Book Stores.

Hawkins, Melba, and Barbara Vandergriff. *Caring for School-age Children: A Church Program Guide.* Nashville: Convention Press, 1986.

Henry, Kay V., and Carol Reddish. *Mother's Day Out Program Guide,* Revised. Nashville: Convention Press, 1981.

The Local Church Ministering Through Emergency Child Care. Memphis: Brotherhood Commission.

"Hurts of Childhood" series by Doris Sanford and Graci Evans. Portland: Multnomah Press. Series of children books dealing with death, divorce, sexual abuse, drug abuse.

"In Our Neighborhood" series by Doris Sanford and Graci Evans. Portland: Multnomah Press. Children's books that deal with issues found in most communities: adoption, AIDS, parental fighting, elderly.

Mind That Child. A video from Gateway Films/Vision Video, 2030 Wentz Church Road, Box 540, Worchester, PA 19490-0540; 1 (800) 523-0226. Shows how to recognize symptoms and find healing for the child who has been sexually mistreated. Practical guidance on how to prevent child abuse.

Garland, Diana. *Precious in His Sight.* Birmingham, AL: New Hope, 1993.

CRISIS PREGNANCY/ UNWED MOTHERS

When a woman or teenaged girl learns that she is pregnant and does not want to be, it is a crisis. Even when the woman is married, if this is an undesired, unplanned pregnancy, it can be a crisis. Unfortunately, pregnancy causes great hormonal change, and the one who is in the midst of a crisis pregnancy must make important decisions while under physical as well as emotional stress.

In today's society, there are four options: abortion, adoption, single parenting, and marriage (for the unwed). The Southern Baptist Convention has adopted resolutions opposing abortion and has developed Alternatives to Abortion Ministries through the Home Mission Board.

A great deal can be done in ministry for expectant mothers to help them make wise choices. Continuing ministry during the pregnancy and after the child is born is important. And there is a great need for ministries to women who chose abortions and are now suffering from emotional, spiritual, and even physical trauma.

Crisis Pregnancy Centers

A crisis pregnancy center (CPC) is a place in a neutral setting, accessible to the general public where a woman can receive a free pregnancy test, confidential counseling, education, and assistance. Many are operated by associations and churches, as well as other nonprofit groups, such as BirthRight. A crisis pregnancy center is distinctive in the type of counseling provided to those who are pregnant and the commitment to assist those who choose to carry the baby to term.

While most centers have a paid director, the rest of the staff are volunteers. Training is essential. Volunteer counselors are required to complete 18 hours of training in crisis pregnancy counseling. Contact your state Baptist convention or the Home Mission Board to learn if there is a crisis pregnancy center in your area.

Crisis pregnancy centers also need:
- Furniture for the center
- Office equipment
- Literature for clients
- Wholesome magazines
- Tasteful decorations
- Toys for children's play area
- Quality maternity and infant clothing
- Baby supplies (diapers, formula, etc.)
- Baby furniture
- Specialty volunteers: maintenance, office help, public relations, printers, computer operators, advertising, professionals such as doctors and lawyers, other advisors and advocates.

For more information about crisis pregnancy centers, contact Alternatives to Abortion Ministries at 1 (800) 962-0851, or write the Home Mission Board.

Housing

Many persons in a crisis pregnancy for various reasons need a place to stay during the pregnancy. Volunteers are needed to provide housing through shepherding homes and as volunteers in group and maternity homes. A shepherding home is a Christian home where a mother-to-be can stay during her pregnancy and for up to six weeks after the birth. She is ministered to by a trained, caring couple.

A group home is a residence where several mothers-to-be live with houseparents during pregnancy. A maternity home provides housing for a larger group of women. Contact your state Baptist convention and crisis pregnancy center to volunteer. Supplies are also needed in these homes, and you or a group may wish to help in this way.

BirthRight operates Welcome Home. Pregnant women are given a place to stay, emotional support, counseling, spiritual guidance, and friendship. Volunteers are needed.

Other Ministries to Unwed Mothers

- Adopt an unwed mother. The woman who chooses to be a single parent no longer faces ostracism from society. However, single women raising children are among the poorest segment of the population economically. Offer personal support, friendship, occasional help with baby-sitting, and spiritual guidance. Or provide one of the following:
  - Sponsor a baby shower for a new, single mom or for an economically disadvantaged mom.
  - Create a quilting or crochet club. Form a group to crochet afghans or make quilts for mothers-to-be and their newborns.
  - Observe Mother's Day. Provide a rose and a baby gift for a single parent. Recognize these births in the church just like any other.
  - Fill Christmas stockings with toiletries and baby items. Give to a crisis pregnancy center or maternity house to distribute.

Postabortion Support

In conjunction with a crisis pregnancy center, or as a separate community ministry, offer a support group for women who are grieving as the result of an abortion. This ministry must be forgiving, supportive of the woman, and geared toward healing.

Education

Many of those who come to a crisis pregnancy center fearing that they are pregnant, are not. The CPC provides education about the biblical view of human sexuality and communicates the values of abstinence until marriage.

However, we must not wait until a crisis occurs to provide this education. While teaching sex education to youth may not seem like a WMU project, it is needed, and must be addressed in the context of Christian values.

Discuss the need with church youth leaders, parents, and age-level organization leaders. Offer group sessions to which youth can bring their friends. Materials for education about human sexuality in a Christian context are available from a number of sources.

Where to Get Additional Help

- Public agencies: Department of Social Services,

School Board, Department of Health and Human Services
•Local chapters of these organizations: Women Exploited by Abortion (WEBA), Salvation Army, Birthright, Youth for Christ.
•National crisis pregnancy information:
   Alternatives to Abortion Ministries—1 (800) 962-0851
   BirthRight—1 (800) 848-LOVE
•State convention and associational church and community ministries directors
•Baptist children's home directors

Resources

Home Mission Board: "What Is a Crisis Pregnancy Center?" (601-01F); "Alternatives to Abortion Ministries (601-02F); "Grace" (601-04F); *Help I'm Pregnant* (video) (601-01P); *How to Establish a Crisis Pregnancy Center* (video).

The Gift of Hope/The Gift of Life: A Volunteer's Guide to Ministry in the Crisis Pregnancy Center (601-03F). This manual of instruction is available only to those being trained as volunteers in a crisis pregnancy center. Contact Alternatives to Abortion Ministries at 1 (800) 962-0851 for further information and to enlist a trainer.

Christian Life Commission, 901 Commerce Street, Suite 550, Nashville, TN 37203-3620; (615) 244-2495. Order a catalog of CLC materials.

Baptist General Convention of Texas: "How to Begin a Crisis Pregnancy Community Ministry."

Baptist Center for Ethics, P. O. Box 22188, Nashville, TN 37202; (615) 383-3192. *The Adolescent Experience: Sex Happens* (cassette tape).

Boothe, Sylvia. *Not an Easy Time.* Birmingham, AL: New Hope, 1990. An easy-to-read book about what to do if you are young, single, and having a baby.

Boothe, Sylvia. *No Easy Choices.* Birmingham, AL: New Hope, 1990. Explores the dilemma of crisis pregnancy.

McDowell, Josh. *How to Help Your Child Say "No" to Sexual Pressure.* Waco: Word Books, 1987. Book and video available.

McDowell, Josh. *Why Waiting Is Worth the Wait.* Waco: Word Books. Video and cassette tape available.

Lester, Andrew. *Sex Is More Than a Word.* Nashville: Broadman Press, 1973.

St. Clair, Barry, and Bill Jones. *Sex: Desiring the Best.* San Bernardino, CA: Here's Life Publishers, 1987.

Durfield, Richard, and Renee Durfield. *Raising Them Chaste.* Minneapolis: Bethany House, 1991.

Lynn, David, and Mike Yaconelli. *Teaching the Truth About Sex.* Grand Rapids: Zondervan Publishing House, 1990.

Facing Reality, a health/sex education text for senior high school students emphasizing the abstinence concept as the healthiest way of living. For a brochure, write to Project Respect, P. O. Box 97, Golf, IL 60029-0097.

Garland, Diana. *Precious in His Sight.* Birmingham, AL: New Hope, 1993.

Taylor, Laurie. *How Could This Happen?* Birmingham, AL: World Changers Resources, 1992.

Martin, Sara Hines, *Meeting Needs Through Support Groups.* Birmingham, AL: New Hope, 1992.

Christian Sex Education Series. Nashville: Broadman Press, 1993.

FAMILIES IN CRISIS

Parenting is hard work. It is a demanding, 24-hour-a-day role and many people find it overwhelming. Abusive parents are often in such need of love and support themselves, they are unable to give it to their children. They often expect their children to nurture them. Volunteers can provide a variety of services to these families which will help to break the abuse cycle and protect the children. Such programs are often administered by local social services agencies and volunteers work in conjunction with professional staff.

Parent Aide Volunteer

A parent aide volunteer can accompany a social worker to the home and spend time with the parent, allowing the social worker to concentrate on the child. Parent volunteers often ask the parent for a cup of coffee, sit in the kitchen, and talk with the parent. Because families today may not have the traditional network of family members to offer emotional support, the parent volunteer fills this role. Other services a parent volunteer may provide include helping with transportation, clinic appointments, and shopping.

Volunteers may be trained as lay-therapists and serve as nonjudgmental, nonauthoritarian counselors for abusive parents. Crisis hotlines also use volunteers in this way. Various names have been given to parent-to-parent programs in communities across the country. In each, the basic premise is that by providing the parent with a friend, a confidant, a counselor, that the parent-child relationship will improve. Many of these parents only know people from other dysfunctional families and have no other model for establishing relationships.

Parent volunteers can often fill the role of surrogate parents to the abusive parents, providing the role models and support they did not have as children. This in turn benefits their children. Parent volunteers demonstrate how to have positive relationships through the friendship and support they offer to parents and families.

Parent Support Group

Start a support group for parents in your community. This is for all parents who feel overwhelmed at times by their kids and would benefit from just being able to talk with other adults regularly.

A support group targeted for single parents could offer many ministry opportunities. Parents carrying the load of parenting, household, and employment responsibilities need an outlet for sharing problems and concerns.

Be sure to arrange child care for parent support groups. Involve concerned adults and older youth who will understand this to be a ministry in itself. Use Big A Club material with the children who come each week with their parents.

Mother's Morning Out

A one-morning-a-week program allows mothers of preschoolers in the community to have some free time for shopping, errands, and relaxation. This ministry offers many witnessing and friend-

ship opportunities. Volunteers staff the program and guide the children in planned activities. A few hours away from the demands of preschoolers can be a great stress relief.

Mom's Alliance

A support system for new mothers, Mom's Alliance pairs an experienced mom with a new mom. Often county social services administers a program, but a church or women's group can also begin one in the community.

First Steps

First Steps is a support group for young parents, ages 14 through 24, and their children. Experienced parents volunteer to offer parenting education, GED, life skills, counseling and friendship.

One community operates the Parenting Place, a drop-in center for young parents. Staffed by volunteers and professionals, it offers a place for young parents to join in a workshop or discussion group, and also have some fun. Infants and toddlers are cared for in special activities while parents have time to learn about employment opportunities, GED classes, or receive help with homework. Contact your county social services department about helping with a program in your community.

Parenting Education

Offer courses in parenting and relationship skills. Or offer a workshop discussing remarriage and blended families. Make these available to the community at large.

Foster Grandparents

This program is generally sponsored by the Department of Aging. Senior adult volunteers work with disadvantaged children who need special care. It is a great ministry for an individual or team.

Family Violence

Family violence, like other problems, is often multifaceted. It often occurs in conjunction with substance abuse, illiteracy, unemployment, and other difficult circumstances. But family violence also occurs in the most "respectable" families. It generally takes one of these forms: physical violence, psychological abuse, sexual abuse (marital rape, incest), and destruction of property and pets.

Contact your local social service agencies for information about intervention programs in your area. As an individual, learn about the shelter options in your community. Volunteer to help. Encourage persons you may know who need to get out of an abusive situation to take advantage of the support and services that are available.

Foster Parenting

Although thought of as a ministry to children, ideally foster care is a ministry to the family. For many reasons, some parents find themselves unable to care for their children. Sometimes a grandparent or other relative will step in to care for the child. Under certain circumstances, social service agencies will remove the child from the home. In all cases, attempts are made to work with the parents with the goal of eventually reuniting the family. Children need special care during this time of upheaval in their lives. Christian foster parents are desperately needed. The case load of social service providers is overwhelming and growing.

Some foster parents balance foster care with raising their own children. Others choose this ministry after their own children are grown. Training is required. Foster parents must also pass a police background check, home inspection, and have a physical. Foster parents are paid a stipend which covers the expenses of having the child in the home.

Where to Get Additional Help

•Public agencies: Family and Child Services, Department of Social Services, Child Protective Services, Battered Women's Shelter
•Local chapters of these organizations: YWCA, Parents Anonymous, Families Anonymous, Toughlove
•National organizations:
National Committee for Prevention of Child Abuse, 332 South Michigan Avenue, Chicago, IL 60604; (312) 663-3520
National Coalition Against Domestic Violence, P. O. Box 15127, Washington, DC 20003-0127; (202) 293-8260.
•National Domestic Violence Hotline: 1 (800) 333-SAFE
•Home Mission Board: Ministry/Witness Resource

Guide: "Families in Stress" (301-18P).
•State convention and associational church and community ministries directors
•Baptist children's home directors

Resources

Channing L. Bete Co., 200 State Road, South Deerfield, MA 01373. 1 (800) 628-7733. Series of scriptographic booklets for family life education. Contact them for a catalog. Booklets cover a wide variety of topics.

American Guidance Service, Inc., P. O. Box 99, Circle Pines, MN 55014-1796. 1 (800) 328-2560. Call for a catalog of resources, including: *Systematic Training for Effective Parenting* (STEP) and *Systematic Training for Effective Parenting of Teens* (STEP/Teen). Supplemental material to STEP and STEP/Teen for teaching practical parenting skills with a Biblical perspective is also available (STEP Biblically and STEP/Teen Biblically).

Serendipity, P. O. Box 1012, Littleton, CO 80160. (800) 525-9563. Bible study/support group series titles for parents:
•*Blended Families: Yours, Mine, Ours*
•*Parenting Adolescents: Easing the Way to Adulthood*
•*Single Parents: Flying Solo*
•*Learning Disabilities: Parenting the Misunderstood*

Stark, Evan. *Everything You Need to Know About Family Violence*. New York: Rosen Publishing Co., 1989.

White, Joe. *What Kids Wish Parents Knew About Parenting*. Sisters, OR: Questar Publishers, Inc., 1991.

Crase, Dixie Ruth, and Arthur Criscoe. *Parenting By Grace*. Nashville: Convention Press, 1986. Parent's Guide, Leader's Notebook.

Langston, Evelyn. *Lord, Help Me Love This Hyperactive Child*. Nashville: Broadman Press.

Smith, Charles. *Helps for the Single Parent Christian Family*. Nashville: Convention Press.

Batten, Joe. *Tough-Minded Parenting*. Nashville: Broadman Press, 1991.

Fulbright, Pat. *Troubled Teens, Troubled Parents*. Nashville: Broadman Press, 1989.

Sorrels, J. Paul, and Libby Potters-Hillyer. *Uniting Generations: A Resource Manual for Intergenerational Ministry.* Nashville: Convention Press.

Family Secrets (My Experience with Family Violence). Birmingham, AL: New Hope, 1988.

Miller, Dorothy. *What Happened?* (My Experience with Divorce). Birmingham,Al: New Hope, 1987.

Stamm-Rex, Lynn. *The Money Trap* (My Experience with Financial Difficulties). Birmingham, AL: New Hope, 1989.

Garland, Diana. *Precious in His Sight.* Birmingham, AL: New Hope, 1993.

Martin, Sara Hines. *Meeting Needs Through Support Groups.* Birmingham, AL: New Hope, 1992.

Bock, Betty. *You Can Make a Difference.* Birmingham, AL: Woman's Missionary Union, 1992.

HOMELESSNESS

The simplest definition of a homeless person is "any person who needs shelter." Shelter is a clean bed and meal. Shelters for the homeless often offer other services as well, but the main intent is a place of protection from the outside elements.

Ministry to homeless persons can be difficult because of the attending problems that have caused the homelessness. Before trying to choose an avenue of ministry, you should understand the categories of persons needing shelter.

1. Persons needing temporary shelter. These people are homeless due to a crisis which can be resolved, such as fire, flood, or natural disaster. Other persons who may need temporary shelter include crime victims who are afraid to return home, or elderly or handicapped persons whose care situation has broken down, travelers who are stranded, migrants, and persons evicted from rental housing or mortgage foreclosures.

2. Persons needing shelter for a longer period of time. These people need shelter long enough to work through their problems and stabilize their lives. This includes battered wives, runaways, those evicted by their families or friends (particularly teens or the elderly), released offenders, deinstitutionalized persons, and persons who have moved from another area.

3. Persons who need continued care on a regular basis: elderly; physically disabled; and mentally ill.

4. Chronically homeless. These are those often referred to as street people. Most are alcohol and/or drug dependent. Many have untreated mental or emotional illnesses.

Shelters

Volunteer your time at a facility that provides services to homeless people (soup kitchens, shelters, day shelters). There are a variety of jobs to be done.

Hostesses assist with coffee, juice, and snacks. They keep the reception area clean and assist the intake volunteers as needed.

Pantry helpers keep the food pantry clean and organized. They mark shelves and sort food as it is donated. They fill food orders and keep records as required.

Clothes closet volunteers sort and hang clothes. They may wash and repair some as needed. They fill clothes orders and/or assist clients in choosing clothing. They assist with clothing drives.

Counselors work directly with clients to determine needs, screen for drugs and alcohol, and make appropriate referrals to other agencies.

Overnight volunteers stay at the facility overnight visiting with clients and helping them on a one-to-one basis.

Other volunteers are needed: cooks, receptionists, office helpers, child-care workers, tutors for school-age children, teachers, doctors, and nurses.

SHELTER DONATIONS

While some shelters are publicly funded, most are run by nonprofit organizations. All shelters have a constant need for volunteers and supplies. Group and individual donations are always welcome. Because some shelters do not cook meals, ask about the types of foods they can use and distribute. Shelters which do not cook meals prefer easy-open, prepared foods which can be eaten at the shelter or taken along by homeless persons.

Check with the shelter director before taking

donations to the shelter. Be sure the items are needed and can be stored. The most basic need is for sheets, blankets, and towels. Some shelters also distribute clothing and furniture. Only donate items that are in good repair and still usable. Don't drop off junk thinking somebody can use it. Unless the facility is prepared to sort and distribute clothing and/or household items, excesses can be a problem.

Include donations of baby-care items, children's clothing, and small toys. Many of the homeless are young children. Diapers, formula, clean plastic bottles, diaper rash medication, baby wipes, and other supplies are needed by homeless families. New and used small toys (in good repair) can be collected to give to the children in a shelter. Toys are needed year round, not just at Christmas. Choose items which can be carried easily by a child such as a doll, stuffed animal, small car, coloring book and crayons, etc. Do not give toys that require batteries or have a lot of small pieces.

Ministry on the Street

Some homeless people will not come to a shelter. Others would like to stay at a shelter, but the shelters are full. To help these people, you must go to them. Organize a ministry to deliver food, blankets, coats, socks, shoes, and gloves to people on the street. Never go alone. This is a team ministry.

Prepare Transient Bags and distribute them directly to street people or provide them to a soup kitchen or shelter to distribute. Each bag should contain easy-open food items such as vienna sausage or potted meat, raisins, granola bars; snack items such as crackers, fruit cups, pudding cups, and chips. Include a plastic spoon. Tracts or Scripture portions may be included, but choose easy-to-read selections since the illiteracy rate among the homeless is high.

If a ministry group in your community is already working with homeless people, find out what assistance they need. In Baltimore, for instance, Inner Harbor Ministry provides two worship services each Sunday for homeless persons. Assisting on a regular basis, even one or two times a year, helps greatly. Many such ministries provide sandwiches and coffee in conjunction with the service. Women's groups could provide the sandwiches several times a year and participate in the services.

Holiday Meals

Organize or participate in a community effort to provide a special meal for homeless persons. Contact community agencies to see if any church or other group is already doing this. Donate food, paper products, or Scripture portions. Spend a Thanksgiving or Christmas Day serving those in need.

Hostess Homes

Consider making a room available in your own home for a person in need of shelter. Organize a network of persons in your community who could help those temporarily in need of shelter. This might be started as a ministry within your own congregation with persons who need shelter due to fire, unemployment, or family problems. With careful screening, hostess homes can be extended to the local community.

Help Night

Volunteers for the Homeless, a nonprofit group in Atlanta started by a concerned Southern Baptist woman, has developed a ministry to those who want to get off the streets for good. Persons are allowed one visit per month. They get a meal, a trip to the clothes closet, 5 minutes in the shower, and a 35-minute counseling session. The ministry has developed to go beyond just helping the homeless survive. They are specifically targeting those who want to change and need help to do it.

Volunteers come primarily from the Wieuca Road Baptist Church although other churches and friends of volunteers are involved. Volunteers sort clothes by size and style, provide meals, work with clients, and refer them to other agencies as needed.

This ministry began as the work of one woman giving out lunches to homeless persons. One person, concerned and willing to find a starting point, can be the catalyst to start a new ministry.

Where to Get Additional Help

•Public agencies: Department of Social Services, Health Department
•Local chapters of these organizations: Salvation Army, YMCA, Travelers Aid
•State convention and associational church and community ministries directors
•Baptist center directors

Resources

Christian Life Commission, 901 Commerce, Suite 550, Nashville, TN 37203-3696. (615) 244-2495. Variety of resources on homelessness and hunger. Contact them for a catalog.

Home Mission Board: "Beginning a Ministry with Homeless People" (632-73F)

Florida Baptist Convention: "How to Begin a Ministry with the Homeless."

Changing Places: A Kids View of Shelter Living. Available for $5.00 from the Arlington Community Temporary Shelter (TACT), P. O. Box 1285, Arlington, VA 22210. Written to be given to children who come to the shelter, it tells the story of eight kids who have lived there. Excellent piece for helping children understand what it is like for a child to be homeless and live in a shelter.

Resener, Carl R., and Judy Hall. *Kids on the Street.* Nashville: Broadman Press, 1992.

Kozol, Jonathan. *Rachel and Her Children: Homeless Families in America.* New York: Fawcett Columbine, 1988.

Grant, George. *Bringing in the Sheaves: Transforming Poverty into Productivity.* Brentwood, TN: Wolgemuth and Hyatt Publishers, Inc., 1988.

Torrey, E. Fuller. *Nowhere to Go: The Tragic Odyssey of the Homeless Mentally Ill.* New York: Harper and Row, 1989.

HOSPICE

Around the world the movement for supportive care for the terminally ill and their families is growing. Primarily, this includes hospice care and bereavement support. Volunteers serve the terminally ill patient and their families in a variety of ways and have tremendous opportunities for ministry and witness. Contact your local hospice group to learn more about volunteer opportunities in your community.

Training is required for volunteers who work with these patients and their families. This training covers hospice goals, services and philosophy, confidentiality, family dynamics, coping mechanisms, and psychosocial issues surrounding terminal illness, death, and bereavement. Volunteers will learn what procedures to follow in an emergency or following the death of a patient, and instruction regarding individual responsibilities.

Most hospice and bereavement programs require that a volunteer be 18 years of age or older. Hospice programs are regulated by Medicare. Regulations cover selection of volunteers, orientation, and continuing education. A current tuberculosis test or X ray is also required to volunteer.

Visiting Friends

These volunteers provide emotional support to the patient and the caregiver. Visiting Friends visit in the home, run errands, provide short respite times for the caregiver, and support the family emotionally, socially, and spiritually.

Other Assistance to the Family

If the person who is dying has children, help with child care may be needed as well as help with household chores and maintenance.

One mother whose husband was dying with cancer had two small children. She said, "Just someone to cut my grass would be a big help right now." Practical ministries are always needed and open doors for sharing Christ.

Bereavement Volunteers

An important area of ministry is that of support to the family after a person's death. This includes the families of the terminally ill who have been a part of the hospice program as well as others in the community. Bereavement volunteers assist with funeral home visitation, monthly telephone calls to the bereaved, or help with support groups.

Bereavement centers and support groups serve hospice families as well as people grieving because of other tragic losses: chronic illness; suicides; accidents; sudden infant deaths; crimes of violence; miscarriages; stillbirths; AIDS; and other unexpected deaths.

Remembrance Ceremony

Many hospice programs have an annual Remembrance Ceremony to remember those who have died in the past year. This is an important service for the families, friends, and volunteers. Church groups are asked to donate flowers and baked goods for this annual gathering.

Where to Get Additional Help

- Public agencies: Local hospital hospice programs, Health Department, Department of Aging, Department of Social Services
- Local nonprofit hospice organization

Resources

Hamilton, Michael, and Helen F. Reid, eds. *A Hospice Handbook: A New Way to Care for the Dying.* Grand Rapids: Eerdmans Publishing Company, 1980.

Chase, Deborah. *Dying at Home with Hospice.* St. Louis: C. V. Mosby Company.

HOSPITALS

Because of their role in the community in the care of the sick or dying, hospitals have long been a favorite site of volunteering. Traditional avenues for volunteer service include the hospital auxiliary and the Candy Stripers program. These programs exist in most hospitals and are good entry points for community ministry.

Waiting Room Ministry

Consult with the hospital administrator or volunteer coordinator about serving coffee or snacks in a waiting room, especially surgical or intensive care waiting rooms. Work out a regular schedule for this type of ministry.

Talk with individuals who are waiting. Offer to pray with them. If children are present, play with them. Provide coloring books and crayons or quilt games. A distraught parent is often so worried that she just cannot focus on the child at this time.

If the general waiting room has a children's area, keep it regularly supplied with crayons, coloring books, puzzles, and small toys. These items have a way of going home with the children.

If your hospital does not have a children's area in the main waiting room or emergency room waiting area, offer to set one up. Provide a children's table, chairs, bookcase, and sturdy toys. As an ongoing project, check the area regularly and keep it supplied.

Collect new and used jigsaw puzzles (easy, medium, difficult) for use in hospital waiting rooms. Puzzles can be placed on a table in the waiting area so that outpatients awaiting treatment or families waiting on loved ones can work together or alone to pass the time. Work with hospital staff and arrange to periodically rotate puzzles and discard any with missing pieces.

Hospital Visitation

Most hospitals prefer to limit visitors to immediate family and close friends. There may be restrictions placed on who can visit and the hours. Consult with the hospital chaplain or volunteer coordinator about this type of ministry. Ask about making/delivering cards to patients as one option. Other small items that are appreciated are writing paper and pens, crossword puzzles and pencils, newspapers, current magazines, hard candy, mints, or fresh fruit (if allowed). Include Scripture portions with cards or gift items.

Balloon/Flower Ministry

Establish a community-based hospital ministry to any family member of anyone in your neighborhood. As soon as you learn of a neighbor or family member who is hospitalized, arrange to deliver a get well balloon or flowers to the patient with a note of concern to the family. Assure the family and the patient of your prayers for them. Include a Scripture portion.

New Mothers

Arrange to present a "Welcome, Baby" pack to new mothers. Include a copy of *Home Life* and/or *Living with Preschoolers*, a Scripture portion or New Testament, and a small baby toy. Other items such as disposable diapers or specially printed diaper shirt could be added. Include a message that this has been provided by your church as a reminder of God's love and an encouragement to raise this new baby in the nurture of a local church. Depending on the size of your local hospital, you might arrange to present one to each new mother, or you could choose to present packs to new mothers in your neighborhood. Check your local paper for birth announcements. Also ask your obstetrician/gynecologist and pediatrician if they will provide names and addresses for this ministry.

Newborn Knit Caps

Contact your local hospital about providing knit caps for newborns. There is a constant need and many hospitals prefer the special touch of hand-made caps.

Pediatric Volunteers

Babies born to drug addicted mothers generally need special attention. Many hospitals enlist volunteers to form a "Cuddle Club." These volunteers spend time in the nursery rocking these newborns and others who need more attention than the staff can provide.

Other volunteers spend time with the children who are being treated in the pediatric unit. These volunteers provide relief for parents who need to get away for a meal or to care for other family members. Many pediatric units have a playroom that is staffed by volunteers. Volunteers play games, read, and help older children with schoolwork.

Hospital Guest Houses

In a number of metropolitan areas, special guest houses such as a Ronald McDonald House have been established for the families of people whose children are hospitalized for extended periods. Contact the guest house director for information about volunteering. Provide inspirational books and magazines for guests. Help with cleaning or other maintenance. Visit with families and offer to pray with them.

Scripture Racks

Provide a Scripture portion rack for a waiting area and keep it stocked regularly. The American Bible Society has many selections reasonably priced.

Ministry to the Family

A person who is hospitalized is often very concerned for the well-being of his or her family and may be quite anxious about this. Do one or more of the following and let the hospitalized person know that these things are being done in order to help relieve anxiety:
- Take care of the children, including before or after school.
- Prepare a meal for the family.
- Baby-sit so a spouse can visit at the hospital.
- Clean house and/or do laundry.

To the hospitalized person, your ministry to the family may be more important than visiting at the hospital. Be on the alert for opportunities with persons in the community who need this type of ministry yet are hesitant to ask. Be sensitive to the need and take the initiative. Few people really respond to the "Call me if you need me" offer of help.

Where to Get Additional Help

- Public agencies: Health Department
- Hospital auxiliary, hospital chaplain

Resources

Anderson, Monnie. *Ideas for Hospital Ministries*. Birmingham, AL: New Hope, 1992.

Justice, William G. *Don't Sit on the Bed*. Nashville: Broadman Press, 1974.

HOUSING

Various projects to build or rehabilitate housing have grown up across the United States. The most well known is Habitat for Humanity which has local chapters nationwide. Volunteers are needed for construction, financial support, and on-site teaching of skills to low-income families. Another important ministry is that of providing lunch to work teams.

Habitat for Humanity does not give houses to low-income families. The families sign mortgages for the cost of the house and make monthly payments. However, these mortgages are lower than most because of the volunteer labor, and they carry no interest. Each participating family must also accumulate 250 to 500 hours of "sweat equity" by working on Habitat projects, their house or others, or by doing committee work.

The families go through a lengthy selection process. They have lived in inadequate, sub-standard housing but are hard working and have the ability to pay a mortgage. The money paid back by recipient families then goes to purchase land and materials for future houses.

Volunteers provide the primary labor for housing projects. Habitat strives to match the abilities and interests of volunteers to the work needing to be done. Habitat also strives to include the teaching of construction skills to volunteers who want to learn. As members of families receiving Habitat houses work beside volunteers, they gain knowledge and develop skills involved in building and maintaining a house.

Volunteers provide their own tools, but tools can be borrowed if necessary. Church groups and other service organizations are encouraged to bring work teams to help with Habitat projects. Contact the local director to schedule a work day. As project calendars are developed, Habitat can tell you what kind of work will be done on a particular Saturday, and what kind of materials and tools to bring. Youth can participate in these groups as well as adult men and women.

Another ministry is that of providing work day lunch for the work teams. Individuals or groups are needed to prepare and serve a hearty lunch to hungry work teams.

Christmas in April

Christmas in April is a national one-day blitz by volunteers to help elderly, low-income, and disabled homeowners make repairs and renovations to their homes. All work is done free of charge with donated materials. Churches, community organizations, and service groups refer individuals to the program.

Contact your county volunteer coordinator to see if Christmas in April has been organized in your area. You can help by volunteering to work that day, enlisting others, or donating materials for home repairs. This is also a possible ongoing ministry that can be done regularly in your community. Organize a team of volunteers with home repair and mechanical skills. Let your county Department of Aging and Social Services know of your availability.

Political Action

Promote tenant ownership programs in public housing units in your community. Studies show that with the introduction of tenant management and ownership, crime and teen pregnancies drop, rent collections increase, living conditions improve, and abuse of property virtually ceases.

Many cities have public housing that has been condemned because it has been virtually destroyed by tenants. Radical changes have occurred in many communities where tenants were allowed to rehabilitate public housing in exchange for ownership and management.

Emergency Assistance

For many low-income families, choices sometimes have to be made between eating, heating, and/or paying the rent or mortgage. Church benevolence ministries often include rent and utility assistance. Some programs are also available through county government or by the utility companies themselves. Include appropriate referral to these programs in church benevolence ministries.

Housing for Older Americans

Because of the increasing need for affordable housing for elderly and physically disabled persons, churches and nonprofit groups are getting involved. Consider the options for housing in your community for the elderly and persons with disabilities. Does the need exist for more affordable housing? Could your church consider this ministry? Begin to explore the need and resources. Order "Housing for Older Americans" (632-20P) from the Home Mission Board to learn how congregations can build, finance, and manage housing for older Americans and persons with disabilities.

Where to Get Additional Help

•Public agencies: Department of Social Services, Department of Aging, Economic Opportunity Council, Community Action
•Habitat for Humanity International, Habitat and Church Streets, Americus, GA 31709-3498; (912) 924-6935. Contact for brochures and a list of regional and affiliate offices.
•Christmas in April * USA, 1225 Eye Street, NW,

Suite 601, Washington, DC 20005; (202) 326-8268. Coordinates annual volunteer project to help low-income, disabled, or elderly persons maintain and repair their homes.

HUNGER

Emergency food pantries, soup kitchens, community lunch programs, shelters, and other programs operate in almost every community to feed hungry people. Opportunities to share the love of Christ are ever present. Volunteers collect and sort food, work with clients, distribute food, serve meals, and visit with the people to provide encouragement and spiritual ministry.

Food Banks

Many communities have developed food banks as resource centers for gathering, storing, and distributing government surplus food, discards from grocery stores, surplus stock from food manufacturers, and canned goods from community food drives. These are then distributed at a nominal cost to church and community food pantries, soup kitchens, and shelters.

Volunteers are needed to collect food as well as sort and distribute it. Youth and older children's groups can assist with collecting and sorting food for a church or community food pantry.

Soup Kitchen

Volunteers are needed to help one day a month, one day a week, or every day cooking and serving food. Volunteer drivers assist with food pickups and deliveries.

One volunteer spends her lunch hour once a week serving beverages in a nearby soup kitchen. There are creative ways to make time if you are willing.

Donate equipment such as coffeemakers, utensils, pots, pans, and cutting boards to a local soup kitchen. Offer to help with office duties or in public awareness of the ministry. Many skills are needed. Use every opportunity to share the hope found in Christ.

Self-sufficiency Program

Provide nutrition and basic food preparation skills for recipients of emergency food. Offer classes in canning and freezing to help people learn how to take advantage of purchasing fresh foods when they are low in cost and keeping them for later use. Teach bulk buying strategies and nutritional tips that will help people provide low-cost, high-quality food for their families.

Teach gardening skills. Many cities offer small plots for families to raise vegetables for their own use. Some vegetables can be raised in container gardens if a garden plot is not available. Self-sufficiency programs help people develop the skills needed to feed themselves.

Church Food Pantry

Start a food distribution ministry with an organized plan for obtaining and distributing food. Establish a criteria of items you would like to give each family or individual that you help. On a regular basis ask certain classes or groups to bring specific items. For example: assign bar soap to the Preschool Department, macaroni and cheese to the Children's Department, rice to the Youth Department, and dried beans to the Adult Department. Ask your age-level missions organizations to bring flour, corn meal, or biscuit mix.

Bread for the Hungry

In conjunction with a communion service or World Communion Sunday (first Sunday in October), ask each person or family to bring a loaf of bread. Ask the pastor to relate this to Jesus as the Bread of Life. Distribute the bread to a local soup kitchen, shelter, or food pantry.

Care Bags

Distribute plastic or paper grocery bags with a list of items needed for your church food ministry or a local shelter or soup kitchen. Set a date for these to be returned. Adults, youth, or children can participate in a churchwide or group project. People will respond more readily if the list is specific and short.

Where to Get Additional Help

•Public agencies: Food Stamp office, Health Department (WIC program), Welfare Office, Department of Aging (elderly nutrition program)
•Community Food Bank
•State Baptist Convention: Inquire about the availability of hunger funds and start up funds for a food pantry.
•State convention and associational church and community ministries directors

Resources

"Hunger: A Manual for Ministry." Memphis: Brotherhood Commission.

Home Mission Board: "Southern Baptists' Response to US Hunger" (360-38F); "Beginning a Food Distribution Ministry" (366-21F); "Ministry/Witness Resource Guide: Domestic Hunger" (301-22P).

Florida Baptist Convention: "How to Begin Food Pantry Ministry."

Christian Life Commission, 901 Commerce Street, Suite 550, Nashville, TN 37203-3620; (615) 244-2495. Produces materials on domestic and world hunger. Contact them for a catalog.

Baptist Center for Ethics: *Building a Social Movement for the Hungry.*

National Student Campaign Against Hunger and Homelessness, 29 Temple Place, Boston, MA 02111; (617) 292-4823.

INTERNATIONALS

An international is a person who has come to the United States for a limited period of time. This may be a few days to several years, depending on the person's situation. The term *international* is used in this way to distinguish between persons who are here temporarily as opposed to immigrants, persons who plan to stay here permanently.

International persons come to the United States for a number of reasons. The most common reasons are: diplomats, business persons here for travelers, vacationers, travelers in transit to another country, airplane or ship crewman, and students.

Internationals can be found in any community, but they are most commonly found in government, trade, education, and health care along with international airports and seaports. Places which are popular tourist attractions also draw many internationals.

The Ministry of Friendship

On a missions trip to Rwanda, Africa, my greatest disappointment was not getting to visit in a Rwandan home. Just as I wanted to visit in a home there, visitors to the United States often want to visit in American homes.

The holidays are a particularly good time to invite internationals into your home. They enjoy learning about American customs and want to be included in our celebrations. Witnessing opportunities abound when we can share the reason for our celebrations.

However, do not limit in-home hospitality to just the holidays. Those who are here for work or studies can be lonely during free time. Hospitality and friendship are welcomed.

Conversational English

Many people study English overseas. But what they often learn is a textbook version of English, not English as it is spoken here. Many can read English, but have difficulty following a conversation. Others, such as spouses of businessmen, have not studied English and find themselves in a strange country, trying to shop and make friends in a language they don't understand.

Check with your chamber of commerce, city planner, local government, local businesses, medical center, or university to learn about internationals in your area. Offer Conversational English classes as an outreach ministry. Offer other activities as your circle of contacts expands.

Contact your Baptist association or state Baptist convention office for the names of literacy workshop leaders. A literacy workshop led by a Home Mission Board certified workshop leader will show prospective tutors how to use the Bible and witness in the Conversational English ministry.

Shopping

Offer shopping trips and classes. Shopping in America can be a frustrating experience for the international visitor, especially one with limited English. This is compounded by differences in units of measure (most of the world uses the metric system), understanding currency exchange, and differences in foods. Just as we have our favorites, internationals have foods they particularly like, and may not be able to find here. Orientation to American grocery and clothes shopping is a real help to the international.

Sight-seeing Through American Eyes

Much of what the international visitor knows about America has been learned through books, television, and movies. Offer to take internationals to points of interest in your area and explain their significance. Express interest and appreciation for what the visitor has learned about America.

Special Occasions

As you get to know your new international friend, find out his or her special days—national holidays, birthdays, anniversaries, etc. Send cards or other greetings on these days and encourage your friend to tell you about their significance. Such dialogue will open doors for sharing Christian faith and the Christian interpretation of many festivals, holidays, and other occasions.

International Banquet

Plan a dinner for internationals in your community or ask them to a food swap of their national favorites. Decorate with flags and items from around the world. Recognize each country that is represented. Use this as an introduction to ministries that you are providing for internationals or as an annual celebration for all who currently participate in these ministries. Encourage internationals you know to bring friends to this event.

Neighborhood Bible Study

As you get to know internationals who are living in the United States for an extended stay, invite them to participate in a neighborhood Bible study for internationals. Many are curious about what Christians believe and would respond to an invitation to study the Bible, even though they may not be believers. Other visitors to this country are Christians, but do not feel comfortable in a regular Sunday School class because their English is not good enough to keep up. They would enjoy a class using materials in basic English and geared to sharing cultural differences as a part of the class.

The Sunday School Board produces quarterly literature for adult Bible study for internationals. Woman's Missionary Union has produced a 12-session basic mission study with biblical content, missionary story, and personal application. This study, *Telling the World About Jesus,* is available in several languages.

Friendship International House

During the days between Christmas and New Year's Day, college dormitories close and many international students have no place to go. Friendship International House (FIH) is a program designed to meet that need and also give international students the opportunity to visit in an American home.

The program is administered by the Student Ministry Department of the Baptist Sunday School Board. Students complete an application indicating their desire to participate and what city they would like to visit from the listing of available sites included in the information they receive. The list of available cities is determined by the number of sponsors that are available.

A sponsor can be a church or association that completes an application with FIH by July 1. The sponsor agrees to enlist host families in the area for as many students as possible that wish to visit that area.

For further information about becoming an FIH sponsor and/or host family, write: Student Ministry Department, Baptist Sunday School Board, 127 Ninth Avenue, North, Nashville, TN 37234; (615) 251-2783.

Other Ministries

See the additional material under "Literacy" (p. 35) and "Seamen's Ministry" (p. 54).

Where to Get Additional Help

•Public agencies: City or county government, city planning office, medical centers, colleges and universities
•Associational church and community ministries directors

Resources

American Bible Society, 1865 Broadway, New York, NY 10023; (212) 408-1200. Order a catalog of materials in Basic English as well as other languages.

Home Mission Board: Ministry/Witness Resource Guide: "Internationals" (301-21P); "Beginning a Conversational English Ministry" (366-33F).

Scripture Distribution, Attention: Jack Roddy, 1350 Spring Street, NW, Atlanta, GA 30367; (404) 898-7441 (7:00 A.M. to 3:45 P.M. eastern time. Answering machine service too.) Call for a complete list of inexpensive Scripture resources, including New Life New Testaments (850-word vocabulary).

Florida Baptist Convention: "How to Begin Literacy Missions: Conversational English."

Baptist General Convention of Texas: "How to Begin Community Ministry to International Families."

Baptist Sunday School Board: Adult Bible Study for Internationals. Bible study for persons learning to speak English as a second language. From "Life and Work" series. Written at reading level six. Quarterly publication (1123-0).

Bible study materials are also available in Korean, Chinese, Spanish, French, Vietnamese, Laotian, Japanese, and Arabic. See the Church Materials Catalog for additional information.

Hunke, Dixie. *Attitudes and Etiquette*. Birmingham, AL: New Hope, 1989.

Snowden, Mark et al. *Meeting the World*. Birmingham, AL: New Hope, 1992.

Merritt. Phyllis. *Telling the World About Jesus*. Birmingham, AL: Woman's Missionary Union, 1991. Undated curriculum unit available in Basic English, Arabic, Laotian, Chinese, French, Korean, and Vietnamese.

LITERACY

Literacy training is divided into two main categories: adult reading and writing (ARW) and English as a second language (ESL). In ARW, tutors work with adults who have limited reading ability. In ESL, tutors teach English to persons whose native language is other than English and who may or may not have previous English training.

Adult Reading and Writing

Tutor training is available through your association or state convention. A 16-hour training workshop will equip you to begin a ministry in your local church. Contact your association or state Baptist convention for the names of literacy workshop leaders. A literacy workshop led by a Home Mission Board certified leader will show tutors how to use the Bible and witness to an adult nonreader while using the Laubach materials to teach reading and writing.

Tutoring is a ministry that can be done by an individual and adapted to suit family and work schedules. You will be called, given some basic information about the prospective student, and asked if you would like to work with this person.

Tutoring can be set up at the church media library, your home, the student's home, or some other place at a time convenient to both of you. The materials are easy to use and step-by-step instructions are provided for the tutor. Community-based organizations also provide training and opportunities for involvement.

English as a Second Language

Similar materials are available for teaching English. This process is a bit more complicated because you are teaching people to speak our language as well as read and write it. ESL, also called ESOL (English for Speakers of Other Languages) by some groups, provides tremendous opportunities for meeting people from around the world and sharing your faith with them.

The Home Mission Board publishes conversational English material based on the Gospel of Mark. This material is preferred by many who would like to use ESL literacy ministry as a witnessing tool. ESL can be taught in groups and advertised in the native language of the target group. ESL is different from ARW in that it focuses more on conversational English. While many of the persons who seek these classes do read and write in their native languages, others are completely illiterate. These must not only be taught to speak English, but how to read as well. ESL is a good way for a church to reach out to an ethnic group in the community or to persons who have come to the United States for a temporary stay.

Contact your associational or state Baptist convention office for information on tutor training using Southern Baptist literacy materials.

Preventing Illiteracy

There are many children at risk of slipping through the cracks of our educational system. Most of these kids need one-to-one help with schoolwork. Volunteer tutors are assigned by the school to work with a student who needs more help. School-based tutors work with students at the school on a schedule arranged with the administration. Other ways to help at-risk students is through after school programs at your church or in other community settings such as Boys and Girls Clubs.

Volunteers may also arrange to tutor a student who lives in their own neighborhood by contacting the school. School administrators will let the parents know of the availability of a tutor and a meeting will be arranged. Tutoring can then take place in the volunteer's home or the student's home on a schedule worked out between the volunteer and the student.

Tutoring a youngster does not require an education degree. Just taking the time to read with a student, help them with their homework, and praise their accomplishments will make a tremendous difference in their schoolwork. You can do this.

Working with Parents and Preschoolers

While many people read to their babies from the time they are very tiny, others never read a book to their children. Perhaps the parents do not read well or do not have appropriate books in the home. When working with people through other ministries such as food pantry, clothing closet, ARW, or ESL, provide simple books for families with young children. Encourage the parents to read to their children and take them to the library. Be sure that

people know that the library is free. If you are providing parenting classes or other support to families, take a trip to the library and introduce parents to the services provided there: story hour, book checkout, films, and cassettes.

Book Bank

Set up and maintain an on-site library, reading center, or book bank in a community without ready access to the public library. This might be in the multipurpose room of an apartment complex or housing development or in a recreation center. Encourage children to read by having a weekly story hour, homework help club, and other activities. Include books for children that present the gospel, teach values, and address the concerns of children.

Special Needs Tutoring

Prisons, juvenile correction facilities, drug and residential rehabilitation centers need volunteer tutors. Many of the people in these facilities cannot read and part of the rehabilitative process includes teaching them to read. In a nonsectarian setting, you may have to use nonreligious materials, such as the Laubach method. However, many opportunities for witnessing will come as you get to know the individual. The Bible can be used later as supplementary reading.

Other Support

Providing transportation, child care, and reading materials are other avenues for supporting literacy ministries. Help staff a literacy office. It is important for those calling to talk personally with a volunteer who is well informed about the program.

Place children's reading materials in the waiting rooms of hospitals, Department of Social Services, and Health Department offices, and other places where a parent may be encouraged to read to a child. Include easy-to-read Scripture portions.

Where to Get Additional Help

•Public agencies: School board, Department of Social Services, public library
•Local chapters of these organizations: Literacy Council, Laubach Literacy Action, Literacy Volunteers of America

• State convention and associational church and community ministries directors

Resources

Literacy: A Vital Mission (A Study Unit and Resource Kit to educate the church about literacy ministry). New Readers Press, Laubach Literacy International, Box 131, Syracuse, NY 13210. 1 (800) 448-8878. Also, contact them for a catalog of tutoring materials using the Laubach method to teach adult reading and writing.

Home Mission Board:
How to Prepare for a Literacy Missions Workshop (632-74F)
Local Church Literacy Needs Survey Guide (632-44F)
Beginning a Ministry with Adult Nonreaders (366-32F)
Beginning a Conversational English Ministry (366-33F)
Literacy Missions: Church and Community (366-02F)
English Lessons from the Bible: Book of Mark, Book 1— Student Edition (632-22P)
English Lessons from the Bible: Book of Mark, Book 1— Teacher Edition (632-21P)
English Lessons from the Bible: Book of Mark, Book 2— Student Edition (632-23P)
English Lessons from the Bible: Book of Mark, Book 2— Teacher Edition (632-24P)
So He May Run Who Reads (632-26P)
That All May Read God's Word (video) (366-08P)

Please contact the HMB for a current listing of literacy materials. At the time of this printing, several literacy products were being revised and some new products were in preparation.

Florida Baptist Convention: "How to Begin Literacy Missions: Adult Reading and Writing"; "How to Begin Literacy Missions: Conversational English."

Public library: Adult Basic Literacy Education (ABLE) collection. These are supplementary materials written to appeal to adults to encourage them to read. Ask your librarian if your library has an ABLE collection.

MENTAL HEALTH

Programs and facilities to help people with mental health problems vary widely. While some people seek help through private counselors and therapists, others are treated in county or state hospitals.

Facilities that care for the mentally ill have a great need for volunteers. Many of the requests are for jobs in the facility such as running the canteen or patient store. Other requests include social activities such as coffee hour, games, and musical entertainment. Patients always enjoy concerts, puppet shows, and other types of programs.

Psychiatric facilities generally limit young children. However, older children and youth can do certain types of seasonal activities such as Easter baskets and Christmas stockings. Children's and youth groups may also provide musical programs, tray favors, handmade cards, or other items with the approval of the activities director.

There is also a great need for support of the families of persons who are mentally ill. Personal ministry to the family could include care of children during therapy sessions, cards expressing encouragement, and a listening ear. Help with groceries or other expenses is also often appreciated if the family is bearing the cost of the treatment. Many insurance programs offer only limited coverage for mental health treatment.

Suicide Prevention

One of the great myths regarding mental health care is that if we don't talk about a problem, it will go away. This is especially true of suicide. Many people fear talking about it will plant the idea in the person's mind. Actually, those who give the warning signals have already thought about it but need the opportunity to ventilate their feelings. The rise in teen suicides, especially those that occur in clusters, has given rise to community intervention programs and telephone hotlines.

Consult with community mental health professionals about starting a teen outreach program that teaches suicide awareness and how to get help for oneself or a friend. Train volunteers (adults and youth) as listeners, who will be the first step in getting appropriate help for troubled teens. Ventilating feelings, to someone who is supportive and is trained to help guide the person to recognize that choices are available, can prevent suicides.

Publicize the availability of your outreach program. Contact school and community leaders. This type of ministry is not a substitute for the work of trained mental health professionals. But it can be the first line of contact for troubled youth. Include activities and programs designed to help build self-esteem and the sense that someone truly cares.

Crisis Phone and Information Lines

Across our nation and around the world the telephone is a vital link between people. People in crisis situations often prefer to talk initially with someone they don't know. Sometimes, they just need to talk to someone so desperately, but they know no one to call. For whatever reason, crisis phone lines have become an important tool in community ministry. While some lines are supervised by professionals, most are staffed by volunteers.

Crisis phone line volunteers receive training to help them respond appropriately to callers. Training varies in length depending upon the organization and type of services offered.

While some lines are national, others are strictly local or regional. Consult your telephone directory for national and local hotlines. Most metropolitan directories gave listings under Hotlines, Crisis Numbers, and Human Service Agencies. Contact one in an area of interest to you and find out how to get involved in the ministry as a volunteer.

If persons in your church or association have expertise in a particular field and there is a need in your community, consider establishing a local hotline. Publicize information about what hours calls will be received. If possible, be sure to have an answering machine to take calls with emergency help information when the line is not staffed.

Where to Get Additional Help

•Family doctor, mental health specialists
•Public agencies: Health Department, Department of Social Services, library
•Local chapters of these organizations: Mental Health Association; Alliance for the Mentally Ill; Recovery, Inc.
• National Organizations:

National Institute of Mental Health, 5600 Fishers Lane, Rockville, MD 20857; (410) 443-4536.

National Mental Health Consumers' Association, 311 South Juniper Street, Suite 902, Philadelphia, PA 19107; (215) 735-2465

National Alliance for the Mentally Ill, 1901 North Fort Myer Drive, Suite 500, Arlington, VA 22209; (703)524-7600.

National Mental Health Association, 1021 Prince Street, Alexandria, VA 22314-2971; (703) 684-7722. Contact them for a listing of publications.
United States Department of Health and Human Services, Mental Health Administration, produces a series of free publications on mental health. Many are available from the Consumer Information Center, Pueblo, Colorado. Or contact the National Institute of Mental Health, Public Inquiries, Room 15C-05, 5600 Fishers Lane, Rockville, MD 20857.
•"Plain Talk About Depression"
•"Plain Talk About Handling Stress"
•"Plain Talk About the Stigma of Mental Illness"
•"What to Do When a Friend Is Depressed"
•*Schizophrenia: Questions and Answers*
•*Caring About Kids: The Importance of Play*
•*Caring About Kids: Learning While Growing*
•*Caring About Kids: When Parents Divorce*

The Information Center, 11036 Ironwood Road, San Diego, CA 92131-1812. Send $1.00 for a catalog of materials on suicide prevention, depression, burnout, grief recovery, enhancing self-esteem, family therapy and other mental health topics. Includes materials for the professional as well as concerned community leaders, family and friends.

Resources

Baptist Book Store—LIFE Courses:
Search for Significance, a study on strengthening one's self-concept. Developed through Rapha, Inc., a provider of hospital treatment centers for psychiatric disorders and addictions.

Making Peace with Your Past, a course dealing with dysfunctions and codependency.

Blackburn, Bill. *What You Should Know About Suicide*. Waco: Word Inc., 1990.

Dickson, Charles. *Please Help Me Hold On*. Birmingham, AL: World Changers Resources, 1992.

Dockrey, Karen. *Curing the Self-hate Virus*. Birmingham, AL: World Changers Resources, 1993.

Dockrey, Karen. *Alone But Not Lonely*. Birmingham, AL: World Changers Resources, 1993.

Esser, Aristide H., and Sylvia D. Lacey. *Mental Illness: A Homecare Guide*. New York: John Wiley and Sons, Inc., 1989.

Hines, Sara Martin. *Meeting Needs Through Support Groups*. Birmingham, AL: New Hope, 1992.

Johnson, Julie Tallard. *Hidden Victims: An Eight Stage Healing Process for Families and Friends of the Mentally Ill.* New York: Doubleday, 1988.

Johnson, Jerry. *Why Suicide?* Nashville: Oliver-Nelson Books, 1987.

Gardner, Sandra and Gary Rosenberg, M.D. *Teenage Suicide.* Englewood Cliffs: Julian Messner (Simon and Schuster), 1990.

Wright, Norman. *Crisis Counseling.* San Bernardino, CA: Here's Life Publishers, 1991.

Grosshandler, Janet. *Coping with Verbal Abuse.* New York: Rosen Publishing Group, 1989.

Daehart, William J. *The Student as Friend in Need.* Nashville: Convention Press, 1992. Teaches students how to minister to other students who are facing crises such as suicide, depression, and loneliness.

Connor, Virginia. *Out of the Darkness* (My Experience with Depression). Birmingham: New Hope, 1988.

Langford, Mary. *That Nothing Be Wasted* (My Experience with the Suicide of My Son). Birmingham: New Hope, 1988.

MIGRANTS

Migrants, the invisible people, the ones who pick the crops and make it possible for the rest of us to eat, are a group often ignored. In the United States they follow three main streams of migration across the country, following the crops as they are ready for harvest.

Churches and associations that include farm land will find this to be a ministry that literally comes to you, yet it is a ministry that will only be done by intentional effort. While migrants may be living in your community for several weeks, they will not visit your church. You must take the church and ministries to them.

Migrants are poor and work long hours for low wages. They have many health problems, are often illiterate, may not speak English, and need to know that God loves them and that others care.

Visiting the Camps

Depending on where you live, this will be a seasonal ministry. It can be a tremendous opportunity for persons who are bilingual, especially in Spanish. To begin, determine when migrants come to your area. Ask farmers when migrants arrive, where they live, and how you could be a help to them. To actually visit the camp you must contact the farmer and/or person in charge of the work group for permission.

A universal point of entry to ministry with adults is ministry to their children. Begin with puppet shows, films, children's activities, and refreshments to create interest. Follow up with adults, encouraging them to attend worship at the camp or at your church (if you provide transportation). Give out Scripture portions in Basic English and/or Spanish. If you discover a worker who speaks another language, obtain a Bible or Scripture portion in the native tongue.

Be sensitive to the needs but realize you cannot change all the problems that face migrants in just a few weeks. Your ministry of concern, of providing some basic resources, and sharing Jesus will mean a great deal to folks who are isolated from much of the rest of society.

Health Kits

Poverty and poor living conditions make even the most basic cleanliness and sanitation a luxury for migrants. Prepare health kits to give each person at the camp. Try to find out in advance about how many people come each year and start early to prepare kits. Children and youth can be involved in gathering and packing the kits as well.

You may sew cloth kits, about 14 inches square with a drawstring top, or use large, resealable plastic bags. Each kit contains: a washcloth, toothbrush, toothpaste, large comb, and bar of soap. You might also include shampoo, razor, shaving cream, and travel sizes of other toiletries. Include a Scripture portion in each kit.

Children's kits should include the same items as regular health kits plus a small, unbreakable toy. If you deliver these to a missionary to distribute, label boxes of children's health kits.

Children's Activity Kits

Prepare activity kits for children that include coloring books, crayons, pencils, children's books, plain or lined paper, and Scripture portions.

Involve all age-level missions organizations in making "Use Me" booklets. Pages inside the booklets contain simple activities such as "Chew Me" with a piece of gum attached, "Color Me" with a crayon attached, "Read Me" with a children's tract attached, or "Enjoy Me" with a piece of candy attached.

Include "Meet Me" and "Write Me" pages. On the "Meet Me" page, the children tell the migrant boy or girl something about themselves and why they made the booklet. The "Write Me" page should include a stamped envelope addressed to the child with paper in the envelope and a pen or pencil attached to the page. The migrant boys and girls are encouraged to write back when they receive the booklet. Here is a sample letter for a "Meet Me" page:

Hi! My name is_________ . I am _____ years old. I attend ________ Baptist Church in *(city)* , *(state)* .

Thank you for the work your family does in helping to raise and gather food. I know Jesus loves me and I know He loves you, too. Please write to me. I would like to know about you.

Sincerely,

____

Although there is a great deal of turnover in the migrant population, many stay on the same pattern and return several times to a particular camp. Regular ministries in migrant camps can create opportunities for relationships over several years.

Health and Dental Services

Migrants likely have no health benefits. Enlist a team to provide basic medical care at the camp. Talk with doctors and nurses who can volunteer their time during the season that migrants are in your area. Arrange a place to set up a clinic at a migrant camp.

Prepare first-aid kits for migrant families. Include antibiotic ointment, bandages, pain relievers for adult and children, cold remedies, cough syrup, and a medicine measuring spoon. Include instructions in both English and Spanish. Make sure all medications have childproof caps.

Tutoring and Literacy

Migrant children move around so much that they often do not start and finish the school year in the same school. But education is desperately needed to give them the skills to improve their lives. Arrange to tutor school-age children. If school is not in session, offer a reading club and learning activities to help children retain skills. Provide children's books that the children may keep.

For adults, provide conversational English and/or literacy classes at night. Although you will not have an extended period of time to work with these folks, teach as much as you can in the time you have. Provide materials that the migrants can take with them.

Transportation

In conjunction with other ministries, offer to provide transportation to shopping centers, grocery stores, doctors, and church services. Migrants have limited resources and may not know where to get the best prices on items they need. Offer to take them to a thrift shop or second-hand store where clean used items are sold. They often travel by truck from job to job and do not have individual transportation. Coupled with the ministry of friendship, this will provide opportunities for sharing faith and meeting needs.

Food Pantry/Clothes Closet

If your church already has a food pantry and clothes closet, take a traveling version out to the migrant camps. Find out in advance how many families are generally in the camp and prepare a bag of groceries for each family packed with staple items. Include baby food and diapers.

Take an assortment of clothing and set up a clothes distribution center at the camp. Or provide transportation to your church to get clothes and food.

Where to Get Additional Help

•Public agencies: Department of Agriculture, Health Department, Department of Social Services
•State convention and associational church and community ministries directors

Resources

Joiner, Barbara. *Count It All Joy*. Birmingham: Woman's Missionary Union, 1991. See the needs of migrants through one who takes her Acteens regularly to lead Bible school and other activities in migrant camps in Baldwin County, Alabama.

Stubblefield, Jerry. *Missions Activities for Men and Boys*. Memphis: Brotherhood Commission. 1987. Pages 29-31 include good ministry ideas for working with migrants.

Home Mission Board: "Beginning a Ministry with Migrant Workers" (366-22F); *Ministry/Witness Resource Guide: Migrants* (301-15P).

MILITARY

The national armed forces are a part of every community. There may be a military installation or reservists in your community. Or perhaps, someone from your community is on active duty elsewhere.

These situations offer ministry opportunities for an individual or a group. Ministry to the military personnel is suitable for adults, youth, or children.

Ministry to Military Personnel from Your Community Serving Away from Home

Learn the names of people from your community who are serving in the armed forces. Many local papers carry news items about people in the community who are in the military. Contact their families to learn their addresses.

Adults, youth, and children can send cards and notes of encouragement to these individuals. Learn their birthdays and other special days. Find out which ones are married and where his or her family is staying. If the family is separated, send notes of encouragement to them as well. Children and youth might become pen pals with a military child living overseas.

Send care packages periodically. Cookies, brownies, and other homemade treats are always welcome. Include a Scripture portion and a note saying that the package is from friends at your church. Pray regularly for these individuals. Tell them you are praying and ask them to send you their prayer requests.

Ministry to Military Personnel Living in Your Community

If there are already military personnel in your church, begin with them. Learn about their needs and the needs of others they know in the military community. Contact the chaplain on the military base. Express your interest and ask how you can be supportive of his work. Because of the necessary formalities in military life, it is better to work cooperatively with a chaplain than attempt to minister "lone ranger" style.

Be sensitive to several areas of need: families under stress, families experiencing long periods of deployment, and single persons. Women's groups and local churches can provide friendship and support in many ways.

Military marriages suffer from a higher than average divorce rate. The stress of frequent moves, long separations, and often difficult work situations takes it toll on military families. Women's groups can focus efforts on ministry to the wives and children of military men through a ladies coffee group, neighborhood Bible study, Backyard Bible Club for kids in base housing, and military wives support group. Many military families are struggling to make it financially and would benefit from a food pantry and clothes closet ministry as well.

The military wife on her own with small children would appreciate help with household maintenance, yard work, and emergencies. Families can befriend and assist a military family while they are in your community.

Adopt a single serviceman or servicewoman. Invite them to your home for a meal, afternoon of fellowship, or holiday celebrations. Learn his/her birthdate and be sure to bake a cake. Contact the base chaplain for information on how to adopt someone you don't know. Military personnel in your church can also provide leads to single persons who need a "family."

Where to Get Additional Help

- Chaplaincy Division, Home Mission Board
- Military chaplains

Resources

Hadley, Donald W., and Gerald T. Richards. *Ministry with the Military: A Guide for Churches and Chaplains.* Grand Rapids: Baker Book House, 1992.

Hadley, Don, and Gerald Richards. *Ministry to Military Personnel*, Seminary Extension Study Guide. Seminary Extension Department, 901 Commerce Street, Suite 500, Nashville, TN 37203; (615) 242-2453.

Home Mission Board: "How to Develop Volunteer Chaplaincy Projects" (320-24F).

MULTICULTURAL MINISTRY

Multiculturalism has become the hot word of the 1990s. Depending upon who is using it, the term carries various shades of meaning for different audiences. In general, it refers to the recognition and even celebration of the ethnic and racial groups that are a part of the cultural tapestry of America. For some, this means maintaining a distinct ethnic and cultural identity. For others, it is the issue of putting the person before race or ethnic background. For still others, it is an issue of empowerment.

Southern Baptists address many of these issues through Language missions and Black church relations. Across our country we study the Bible in over 100 languages and dialects each week. More than 6,000 language/culture congregations are affiliated with Southern Baptist work. Yet there is much to be done in confronting racism, eradicating ethnic stereotypes, and addressing the particular needs of ethnic and racial groups in the country.

Language/Ethnic Ministries

Consult your county planning office to learn about language/ethnic groups in your area. Do most live in communities with other persons of the same ethnic/language background or are they scattered throughout the community? Are there particular community leaders of ethnic groups that you could contact?

Provide Scripture portions or Bibles in the languages of ethnic groups in your community. Use some common distribution points like laundromats and hospital waiting rooms. Get permission to set up a "Free—Take One" stand or wall rack. Enclose information about Bible study or worship for this language group in the particular language as well as in English. An English-speaking person might also pick it up, see the invitation, and take it to someone she knows who speaks that language. Include a number to call for more information, emergency assistance and/or Conversational English classes.

Multicultural Fair

If there are a number of ethnic, language, or racial groups in your community, invite persons and groups to participate in a multicultural fair at your church. This could be an outdoor event. Use ethnic art, music, crafts, and food. Promote this as a community get-acquainted or cultural celebration event. Set up an entertainment schedule, display booths for selling crafts and food, and information booths about community services. For your church booth, order Scripture portions and tracts in the languages that will be represented. Give these away free.

Tutoring Can Go Both Ways

Children from language or ethnic backgrounds may need help with schoolwork, especially if the parents do not speak English. Arrange to tutor children in your neighborhood. Or let them tutor you in their language.

One community is working to overcome cultural barriers by having Hispanic students tutor teachers in Spanish. Not only is this self-esteem building for the youth—they can teach the teachers—but it also helps the teachers see the students in a new light. All women's groups can take this lesson to heart in attempting to cross cultural barriers. We must be willing to learn too!

Begin with Other Christians

Arrange for a multicultural Bible study, worship service, or pulpit exchange with an ethnic or language congregation in your community. This does not have to be a Baptist congregation. Dialogue with leaders about your concerns for working together to solve community problems and meet needs. Avoid the use of the word *help* as in "We want to help you." When an Anglo uses it with an African-American or ethnic person, it may be taken as an expression of superiority. Talk about working together instead. Use the contacts that result from this dialogue or other joint endeavor to begin reaching others in the community.

Where to Get Additional Help

•Public agencies: Department of Social Services, City Planning Office
•Ethnic community groups, churches
•Associational director of missions
•Associational and state language missions directors

Resources

Home Mission Board

Black Church Extension: *A Manual for Volunteers in the Black Community* (362-06F); *Churches Ministering to Black America* (362-14F); "Interracial Joint Committee" (362-11F); "Beginning a Companion Church Relationship" (362-12F); *Rev. Dull Visits a Black Church* (362-18P)—humorous account of mistakes often made by Christians communicating across racial and cultural barriers.

Language Church Extension: Working with Europeans (350-05F0); "Working with Hispanics" (350-06F); "Working with American Indians" (350-11F); "Working with Asians" (350-69F); "Working with Pacific People" (350-70F); "Working with Middle Easterners" (350-71F); "Working with Caribbeans" (350-72F); "Guide to Establishing Ethnic Ministries and Congregations" (350-33F).

Scripture Distribution: (404) 898-7441. Call for a complete listing of inexpensive Scripture resources.

Baptist Book Store: Clip Art for African-American Churches (4359-28). Features African-American art for use in newsletters, fliers, and bulletins.

Hunke, Dixie. *Attitudes and Etiquette*. Birmingham, AL: New Hope, 1989.

Snowden, Mark et al. *Meeting the World*. Birmingham, AL: New Hope, 1992.

MULTIHOUSING MINISTRY

The Home Mission Board defines multifamily housing as "any housing with six or more units per acre." This includes apartments, condominiums, mobile homes, marinas, and cluster housing. Multifamily housing dwellers may be poor or affluent. Some are single; others are part of families. Many hope to one day own a traditional single-family home; others prefer the amenities and relief from yard and building maintenance. Thus, it will take various avenues of ministry to reach people in multifamily housing. Contact managers before attempting any ministry.

Study the multifamily unit carefully before launching a ministry. Well-to-do complexes will have differing needs from middle class or poor units. Yet, there will be many of the same needs in any multifamily housing development. Children need attention; parents need a safe place to share frustrations; and youth need guidance no matter what the economic status. However, a bag of groceries and rent assistance may open more doors in public housing, and a seminar on income-tax strategies may garner more interest in a middle-class or affluent neighborhood.

Plan your ministry based on the needs you find. People will respond more readily to the gospel in a context of concern for the whole person or family.

Prepare welcome packets with information about the community. Include maps, brochures, tourist information, etc., as well as information about your church and unique ministries that you may offer, such as child care, mother's day out, and Conversational English. Either ask the management to give these to every new family or ask the manager to give you the names and move-in dates of new residents. Then visit in person and deliver welcome packets.

On-site Activities

Many of the same activities described in the sections on children and youth, families in crisis, and addiction ministry can be taken to the multifamily housing site. Recreation, seminars on current topics, support groups, crafts, and children's activities can open doors. Ministry to children will often be the key to reaching a family.

If the multifamily unit has a common or recreation area, ask permission to hold activities there. Take time to build a good relationship with the management, stressing your desire to work together. In those facilities that have experienced problems with vandalism, unsupervised children, alcoholism, and drugs, managers will be more receptive if they can see a benefit for themselves and their complex. Stress that there will be no cost involved for the facility and that you will provide leadership and materials.

Seasonal Activities

Plan appealing community events such as Thanksgiving dinner, Christmas caroling, children's costume party (Halloween), or Easter egg hunt. Provide a program, games, or other entertainment, and refreshments. Give out Scripture portions, including Scriptures for any language groups that might live in the development. Use community wide events as an introduction to other ministries Conversational English, tutoring, and parent support groups.

Where to Get Additional Help

•Public agencies: Housing Authority, Department of Social Services
•State convention and associational church and community ministries directors

Resources

Home Mission Board
Beal, David. *Opening Doors to Multifamily Housing* (312-18P). A complete step-by-step manual for starting and maintaining multihousing ministry.
Perry, Robert L. *Models of Multifamily Housing Ministry* (304-01p).
Bunch, David, Harvey J. Kneisel, and Barbara Oden. *Multihousing Congregations* (3-00-02P).
Ministry/Witness Resource Guide: Multifamily Housing (301-17P).

Baptist State Convention of North Carolina, Church Extension Department, 1 (800) 395-5102, ext. 341. Contact them for a copy of these brochures: "Activities for Your Apartment Community at No Cost to You!"; "Are You Fired Up or Burned Out?"

Amberson, Talmadge R. *Reaching Out to People*. Nashville: Broadman Press, 1980. Deals specifically with reaching people in apartment complexes and mobile-home parks.

NEW AMERICANS: IMMIGRANTS/REFUGEES/ UNDOCUMENTED PERSONS

People come to America from all over the world. Many come for extended visits, but with no intention of settling here permanently, so we refer to them as internationals. Immigrants are those persons who come with the intent of making this country their permanent home.

Some immigrants are refugees who are fleeing their homelands due to persecution, political danger, or invasion. Others come by choice seeking a better life, greater personal freedom, or because they are related to Americans or other immigrants. Most need assistance in getting adjusted to life in this country.

The total number of immigrants per year is controlled by the Immigration and Naturalization Service of the US government. Some people are here illegally and this presents additional problems and issues to be dealt with by those who minister.

Prepare for Cross-cultural Ministry

Misunderstandings occur when we fail to understand cultural differences. Things like shaking hands or hugging are not acceptable in some cultures. Although immigrants will need to learn about American customs, to reach them with the gospel we must learn about their culture and customs first. Study books about the culture and religions of immigrants and internationals in your community. This will help you avoid behaviors that might be offensive. In time, as your relationship with these friends builds, you can explain American customs and dialogue about differences in culture and faith.

Meeting the Immediate Needs First

Many immigrants and refugees arrive here with only a few personal belongings. Even if they are coming to join extended family already here, that family may not be in any real position to help them. Food, clothing, and a place to stay are immediate needs.

Many immigrants live in overcrowded apartments or mobile homes. One apartment manager tells of finding three queen-size beds, four twin beds, and 15 toothbrushes in one unit.

Women's groups, churches, and other groups can become sponsors for a refugee/immigrant family. Sponsors provide food, clothing, transportation, and help secure employment.

Teaching English and Job Skills

Many immigrants do not know enough English to shop, get jobs, open bank accounts, or handle legal documents such as apartment leases. Offer English as a Second Language classes in your community for immigrants. Some immigrants are illiterate even in their own language and will need to be taught reading and writing skills, in addition to learning to speak English.

Be alert to persons who are reticent to give you their name or address. If they are here illegally, fear of deportation is a big issue. Build trust and at the appropriate time, help them take the necessary steps to gain legal entry to this country.

Provide transportation to English classes and/or arrange to have them in the community where the immigrants live.

As language skills improve, help those who need additional education take advantage of community resources and GED classes. Offer classes that teach money management, shopping skills, and other basics needed for survival in America.

Citizenship Classes

In order to become an American citizen, immigrants are required to complete the naturalization process. Persons desiring citizenship must be able to read, write, and speak English, and have a knowledge of US history and government.

Contact your local school board or the US Immigration and Naturalization Service about the availability of citizenship classes. Provide a place if needed and/or teach the required material.

Obtain "Basic Guide to Naturalization," Form M230 from the Superintendent of Documents, US Government Printing Office, Washington, DC 20402. Additional information may be obtained from Immigration and Naturalization Service in your area.

Where to Get Additional Help

•Public agencies: Department of Social Services, Housing Authority, City Planning Office
•Local chapters of these organizations: Literacy Council, Salvation Army
•Associational director of missions
•Associational and state language missions directors

Resources

Baptist General Convention of Texas: "How to Begin a Church Ministry to Undocumented Immigrants."

Home Mission Board
Guide to Establishing Ethnic Congregations and Ministries (350-33F).
How to Sponsor a Refugee (350-109F).
Sponsor of Liberty (350-99F). Sponsorship guide.
Sponsors of Liberty (video) (350-37P).
Great Expectations (350-104F). Deals with the issue of hurt feelings when a refugee's expression of gratitude does not meet the church's expectations.
Cast Out Your Net (350-107F). Order form for refugee awareness materials.
Working with Europeans (350-05F).
Working with Hispanics (350-06F).
Working with Asians (350-69F).
Working with Pacific People (350-70F).
Working with Middle Easterners (350-71F).
Working with Caribbeans (350-72F).

Order a catalog from the Home Mission Board for a complete listing of language materials.

Hunke, Dixie, *Attitudes and Etiquette*. Birmingham, AL: New Hope, 1989. Provides basic information about seven large ethnic groups and gives witnessing suggestions.

Snowden, Mark et al. *Meeting the World*. Birmingham, AL: New Hope, 1992.

NURSING HOMES

Nursing home ministries have two basic needs: group activities and one-to-one visitation. *Ideas for Nursing Home Ministries* has many suggestions for group and individual activities, including Bible study material, seasonal activities, and guidelines for visiting. It is a resource piece that will help you develop a ministry that fits the need in a nursing home facility in your community.

Julia Dooley of Linden, Texas, developed an interdenominational, multichurch Adopt a Hall ministry from a seed idea in *Ideas for Nursing Home Ministries*. She shares her experience here in the prayerful hope that others will adopt a similar strategy for making sure that every resident in a nursing facility receives the ministry of a church or group of committed Christians. Her strategy is another example of the fact that people will respond when the request for help is specific.

Adopt a Hall

Many residents are unable or unwilling to attend activities that are offered by a nursing home. In order to reach them, organize a visitation ministry that assigns individuals, groups, or churches a specific hall to visit, get to know the residents, and be responsible for one-to-one visitation with those residents who do not participate in other activities.

Contact the activities director for permission and guidance in organizing this ministry. Set a time and place for an informational meeting, preferably at the nursing home itself. Contact other churches in your community about getting involved. Include some of the ideas for ministry that they can do on their hall, such as cards, gifts, and in-room ministry. Explain that the number of assigned residents is determined by the number of churches that volunteer to take part in the Adopt a Hall ministry.

Prepare for the first meeting with prayer. Determine how many churches/groups/individuals you will need to minister adequately on all the halls of the nursing home in your community. Pray that God will provide.

At the first meeting share your vision for an Adopt a Hall ministry. Sing several hymns about ministry. Include a message about ministry by a pastor or nursing home chaplain. Ask the activities director to explain the need for this type of ministry. Some groups or individuals will come prepared to make a commitment; others will need to take information back to their churches.

Have a second meeting to finalize the commitment to participate and organize. If this is an interdenominational or associational ministry, some structure with officers or a planning team would help the group work together and assign responsibilities. At the least, one person will need to serve as coordinator. Plan for representatives from each church to meet together occasionally for idea sharing, training, information, and inspiration.

Funding for Adopt a Hall could be handled in one of two ways:

1. Each participating church/group covers the cost of cards and small gifts for persons on their hall. If there is someone on the hall with a special need (clothing, shoes, etc), the assigned group takes care of it.

2. Establish a treasury for the Adopt a Hall ministry to assist with needs of those residents who have no family or are unable to supply such things as clothes, shoes, personal items, etc. The funds may also be used for cards and other items sent to all residents. Cards contain an insert listing all the churches or groups participating in the ministry. Each participating church or group would be asked to make a contribution toward expenses of the overall ministry.

Get pastors involved, too. Ask pastors from participating churches to visit residents on the assigned hall and to help occasionally with worship services at the facility.

Personal Items You Can Provide

Toothbrushes	Stockings (thigh-high nylons)
Toothpaste (for sensitive gums)	Body lotion
Notepaper and stamps	Knee socks or bed socks
Emery boards	Talcum powder or deodorant powder
Cologne (men's or women's)	Dental floss
Christmas cards (new)	Deodorant (roll-on)
Special occasion cards (new)	Soap
Yarn, lace, and craft material	Facial tissues
Pens and pencils	Denture cleanser
Hairbrushes	Hairnets
After-shave lotion	Hair spray
Shaving cream	Hypoallergenic blush and lipstick

Nail polish   Solid-colored
                                  scarves

Residents enjoy homebaked items to go with coffee, tea, or other beverages served in the morning or afternoon. Many facilities have a coffee hour or coffee cart that makes the rounds through the halls at a set time. Consult with the activities director about appropriate items to bring.

Never bring hard candy to a resident without consulting the activities director or nurse first. Choking precautions must be taken with many of the residents. Always ask first.

Pets on Wheels

Your county department of aging may have an established Pets on Wheels program already set up. Contact the activities director and/or the department of aging to inquire. Volunteers visit the nursing home for one hour a week with a pet and make group and in-room visits.

To participate, most programs require volunteers to attend an orientation program prior to visiting. The orientation covers the nursing home environment, the aging process, nursing home do's and don'ts, hints for successful visiting, etc. Pet owners must have the pet screened for suitability of temperament and submit a current health certificate for the pet.

Children can participate in this program with their parents. Nursing home visitation is an excellent way to teach young children to be concerned for others.

One Person Can Make a Difference

You may be the only one in your group who is interested in this ministry. Contact the activities director and offer your services. She might need assistance with a particular activity each week or month. She might have several residents who never receive visitors that she would like to assign to you. If you could come at mealtime, assistance is always needed with feeding residents who cannot feed themselves. The list is endless.

Report to your group or church regularly about your ministry. Express your enthusiasm and invite others to go with you. Be specific. Set the day, time, and what you will be doing. Some will want to go once just to see if they like it or not. Many will be more comfortable going with you than going alone.

When a specific need arises at the facility that your church or group could meet, share the need. Many who cannot visit will participate in collections or one-time events such as a Christmas party.

Where to Get Additional Help

•Public agencies: Department of Aging, Health Department
•Local chapter of American Association of Retired Persons.
•Associational church and community ministries director

Resources

Home Mission Board: "Beginning a Ministry in Nursing Homes" (366-30F).

Bolton, Joy Luebbert. *Ideas for Nursing Home Ministries*. Birmingham, AL: Woman's Missionary Union, 1990.

Bock, Betty. *You Can Make a Difference*. Birmingham, AL: Woman's Missionary Union, 1992.

McCormick, Tom, and Penny McCormick. *Nursing Home Ministry*. Grand Rapids: Zondervan Publishing Corp., 1987.

Manning, Doug. *The Nursing Home Dilemma: How to Make One of Love's Toughest Decisions*. New York: Harper and Row, 1985. An excellent book for understanding the needs of the resident and the family as they adjust to the nursing home environment. Manning explores making the decision, adjusting to the decision, and living with the decision.

Klim, Mary Kay. *Bible Studies for Senior Citizens*. Order from Potentials Development for Health and Aging Services, Inc., 775 Main Street, Buffalo, NY 14203. Ask for a catalog of books, cassettes, videos, games, party ideas, exercises, and other materials for working with nursing home residents.

PEOPLE WITH DISABILITIES

The Americans with Disabilities Act became law on July 26, 1990. It was enacted to give civil rights protection to individuals with disabilities. It guarantees equal opportunity for individuals in public accommodations, employment, transportation, state and local government service, and telecommunications.

The enactment of this law has given heightened awareness to the needs of persons with disabilities and our responsibility to them as a society. However, persons with disabilities especially want to be seen simply as people. As you minister to persons with disabilities, construct your sentences so that the word *person, friend, citizen, student,* etc., comes before the word for a disability. Focus on the person not the disability.

In many communities, persons with disabilities have organized themselves into self-advocacy groups to support one another and address problems. Many of these groups call themselves People First organizations.

Physically disabled

Ministry to persons with physical disabilities includes those who are blind or deaf, and have various problems with mobility. Sometimes physical disabilities are also coupled with developmental disabilities. Many of the schools and social service agencies that provide education and services to persons with disabilities are in dire need of volunteers. In such settings, it is possible to build friendships and have many opportunities to witness.

Some services to persons with physical disabilities are provided through community agencies and schools which focus entirely on the special needs of these students. Contact your county government office to learn about the special services and programs for persons with disabilities in your area and inquire about the need for volunteers.

Even youth and older children can volunteer. One of the greatest needs of all people is friendship. Many persons with physical and mental disabilities feel isolated. The ministry of friendship, one child to another or one adult to another, is often the greatest ministry we can have. In one school, children give up one recess each day to help in the special education class. The main purpose is friendship. In those situations where a child truly becomes friends with a youngster with special needs, marvelous progress has been made and the self-esteem of the child with the disability has soared. The ministry of friendship cannot be stressed too highly.

SCHOOLS

Special schools for the persons who are blind and/or physically disabled can be found in many communities. Some are residential; others are day schools only. Volunteers can work directly with the students or may help with administrative work. Volunteers are often needed for these positions:

Aquatics aide	Swimming assistant
Office assistant	Driver
Tutor	Housekeeper
Classroom assistant	Administrative assistant
Computer instructor	Photographer
Dental assistant	Supply clerk
Reader	Typist
Vocational Aide	Purchasing assistant

INDIVIDUAL ASSISTANCE

Many persons with disabilities can work, live alone, and generally function as any other person with just a little assistance. Volunteers are needed to read to a person who is blind, interpret for a person who is hearing impaired, drive, and assist with shopping or housekeeping needs. The ability to live independently is very important to the person with a disability. While a few communities provide attendant care, it is limited or nonexistent for many. Volunteers can fill the gap. The assistance of friends and volunteers can make what would otherwise be impossible, a reality.

HOME AND HOSPITAL PROGRAM

Some communities have developed programs to teach or tutor homebound and hospitalized students who have physical or emotional impairment. Contact your local school district about the need for volunteers in this type program as a reader, teacher, visitor, or friend.

SIGN LANGUAGE TRAINING

A definite step we can take in ministry is to learn sign language, even if we do not currently know a person who is hearing impaired. Like talking any other language, learning sign language before you need it will prepare you for the unforseen circumstance of needing to help a person who is deaf. Contact your school district office, local social service agency or your Baptist state convention language department to find out where you could get sign language training.

MATERIALS FOR PERSONS WHO ARE VISUALLY IMPAIRED

Provide subscriptions to taped materials such as *Royal Service* for a blind person in your community. Take a friend who is blind to the library to select books and other materials that are available on tape. Prepare your own cassette tapes of materials that he or she would like to have that may not be available on cassette. Bible study and other materials are available on cassette from the Baptist Sunday School Board.

MATERIALS FOR PERSONS WHO ARE HEARING IMPAIRED

Be aware that there is disagreement in the deaf community about the best approach for teaching and translating. Many hearing people do not realize that American Sign Language (ASL) is not a straight translation of English, but is a language with its own syntax and grammar. Materials in basic English are preferred by many people who are deaf. Give a friend a copy of the Bible prepared for persons who are deaf. Also, Sunday School literature and some WMU materials are prepared in basic English.

Developmentally disabled

Persons with mental retardation learn at a slower than average rate. Community organizations such as ARC (Association for Retarded Citizens) are committed to providing assistance to persons with mental retardation. Volunteers can assist in a variety of ways.

RESIDENTIAL PROGRAM

This program provides services to people who are mentally retarded. It provides the residents experiences in daily living which approximate the choices open to other citizens. This may include supervised living in an apartment or house setting with staff and volunteers assisting with cooking, employment, recreation, laundry, and other personal living skills.

INFANT STIMULATION PROGRAM

This community-based program provides developmental stimulation to children, ages newborn to three, who are mentally retarded or have other developmental disabilities.

SHELTERED WORKSHOP

A sheltered workshop provides employment for adults who are mentally retarded in a structured and supportive environment.

RESPITE CARE PROGRAM

Provides short periods of relief for families who provide in-home care for persons who are developmentally or physically disabled. Provides in-home or out-of-home care.

The National Council on Aging (NCOA) has developed the project Family Friends. This links a senior adult to a family with a severely disabled child. It provides friendship to parents and siblings and respite care.

Women's groups could participate in this program or start a similar ministry in the community.

LEISURE ACTIVITIES

Persons who are mentally disabled enjoy leisure activities with others in the community.

VACATION PROGRAM

A vacation program provides opportunities for persons who are disabled to enjoy weekend trips and/or week-long vacations with their peers.

THE MINISTRY OF FRIENDSHIP

Children and adults who are developmentally disabled desire to be included in normal living activities. Include persons with disabilities in any activity in which they can safely participate. A volunteer could take an adult who is disabled with her to visit at the nursing home. This is a double ministry. The special friend is thrilled to be included and does well in this setting. Many persons with Down syndrome, for example, are very loving and open. The elderly in the nursing home enjoy the attention that a person with a disability will lavish upon them. Everybody benefits.

To include a person who is disabled in settings like this requires patience and perhaps some other special arrangements. The ministry of friendship is a great gift. A volunteer can often minister by simply arranging to pick up a friend from a group home for Saturday shopping, Sunday church, or a family meal.

Where to Get Additional Help

•Public agencies: Public school system, Health Department, Department of Social Services, Recreation Department
•Local chapters of these organizations: Association for Retarded Citizens, Special Olympics, National Easter Seal Society, Muscular Dystrophy Association, Learning Disabilities Association
•National Federation of the Blind, 1800 Johnson Street, Suite 300, Baltimore, MD 21230-4998
•American Association on Mental Retardation, 1719 Kolorama Road, NW, Washington, DC 20009-2683; 1 (800) 424-3688

Resources

Disability Bookshop, P. O. Box 129, Vancouver, WA 98666-0129. 1 (800) 637-2256. Send $2.00 to order a catalog of books, videos, and other materials covering a wide range of disabilities and how-to helps.

National Easter Seal Society, 70 East Lake Street, Chicago, IL 60601. (312) 726-6200. Request a catalog of publications and price information.

Baptist Sunday School Board: Adult Sunday School materials are available on cassette tapes. For ordering information, call 1 (800) 458-2772.

Home Mission Board: "Blind Persons" (366-15F); "Disabled Persons" (366-28F); "Beginning a Ministry with Disabled Persons" (366-19F); *Ministry/Witness Resource Guide: Blind* (301-16P); "Working with the Deaf" (350-03F); "Language of Signs" (350-01F); "How Accessible Is Your Church?" (632-42F).

Baptist General Convention of Texas: "How to Begin a Church Ministry to the Blind"; "How to Begin Mission Ministries with Deaf Persons"; "How to Begin a Church Ministry for Disabled Persons."

Perske, Robert, *Circle of Friends: People with Disabilities and Their Friends Enrich the Lives of One Another*. Nashville: Abingdon Press, 1988.

Bergman, Thomas, *On Our Own Terms: Children Living with Physical Disabilities*. Milwaukee: Gareth Stevens Children's Books, 1989.

Jernigan, Kenneth, ed. *What Color Is the Sun?* Baltimore: National Federation of the Blind.

"Guidelines for Reporting and Writing About People with Disabilities." Order from the Research and Training Center on Independent Living (RTC/IL), 4089 Dole, University of Kansas, Lawrence, KS 66045; (913) 864-4095. One copy will be sent free upon request and will include an order form and price information for multiple copies.

Resources for ministry to persons who are deaf
Baptist Book Store
Yount, William R. *Be Opened! Manual for Helping Churches Minister to Persons Who Are Deaf*. Nashville: Convention Press, 1976.

Riekehof, Lottie. *The Joy of Signing*, Revised. Springfield, MO: Gospel Publishing House, 1987.

Holy Bible, English Version for the Deaf. Grand Rapids: Baker Book House, 1989.

Cooper, John A., comp. *Working with Deaf Persons in the Sunday School*. Nashville: Convention Press, 1982.

Survival Kit for New Christians (Basic English). Nashville: Convention Press.

Woman's Missionary Union materials in Basic English
Merritt, Phyllis. *Telling the World About Jesus*. Undated curriculum unit. Birmingham, AL: Woman's Missionary Union, 1991.

Available from Woman's Missionary Union, SBC
The History and Purpose of Home Missions
Biographical Sketch of Lottie Moon

Our Missions World. Targeted to readers who speak English as a second language or who are deaf (available in English, Chinese, and Korean). (monthly)

Resources for ministry to persons who are blind
Home Life Digest (monthly cassette). Nashville: Sunday School Board.

Open Windows (three cassettes, quarterly). Nashville: Sunday School Board.

Royal Service for the Blind (monthly cassette). Birmingham: Woman's Missionary Union.

Resources for ministry to persons with mental handicaps
Ministering to Families with Retarded Members (video). Nashville: Sunday School Board

Teaching Adults with Mental Handicaps in Sunday School. Nashville: Convention Press.

Teaching Children and Youth with Mental Handicaps in Sunday School. Nashville: Convention Press.

PRISON MINISTRY

Security is the primary concern of jail, prisons, and detention centers. Thus, going in as a volunteer can be an involved process. To begin work in a prison, contact the prison chaplain or volunteer coordinator and find out how to obtain a security clearance. Learn what activities are already being done. Decide whether it would be better to help with an existing program or start a new one.

Studies show that prisoners who receive religious training while in prison are less likely to be repeat offenders. This is a demanding ministry, but certainly one that provides long-term benefits to society and eternal benefits to the prisoner whose life is changed by the gospel.

One-to-One Visitation or Correspondence

Through the chaplain or volunteer coordinator, volunteers can be matched with an inmate to visit or write on a regular basis. Initially, one should work to become a dependable friend to the inmate. Over time, opportunity for sharing Christ and ministering to the inmate's family may arise. No contact should be made with the family except at the request or with the permission of the inmate.

Family Ministry

This type of ministry is best done by a husband/wife team or a person of the same sex as the inmate's spouse. Through this ministry, volunteers provide support and friendship to the families of inmates. Initial contact for this type of ministry should be made by the inmate to his family or by the prison chaplain or volunteer coordinator.

Ministry to the families of inmates may include food and clothing assistance, counseling, tutoring, observance of birthdays and holidays, transportation, help for family members seeking employment, and child care. If the family is responsive, include them in church activities and provide Bibles and other Christian literature. Always be ready to share Christ.

Education and Job Training

Tutors to teach nonreaders and the functionally illiterate are needed. Tutoring generally requires a commitment of 1½ hours per session twice a week to work one-to-one with an inmate.

Volunteers can also help inmates prepare for the GED test. This does not require a teaching degree, just a willingness to work with one or two students. Math and English tutors are especially needed.

Job training is perhaps more difficult and must be done in consultation with the prison staff. Many professions are closed to persons with criminal records. However, training in basic skills will go a long way to helping inmates find employment following their release.

Sewing

Would you like to glorify God and "sew" the gospel into the hearts of women? You can! Arrange to visit weekly, biweekly, or monthly and teach sewing or crocheting to female prisoners. During this witnessing time, speak individually with each woman and write down her prayer requests. At the conclusion, pray with the women. Provide Bibles and other Christian literature for them.

Ministry to People with Disabilities

Contact the prison chaplain to learn if there are prisoners who are deaf, physically disabled, or mentally retarded. Arrange for someone to visit these persons in particular and work with them. Persons with disabilities will need individual ministry geared to meet their needs.

Leisure Activities

Prisoners have lots of time and little outlet for using it productively. Many will come to an activity just to have something to do or to get other privileges. They may be hostile and uncooperative. But through consistency and patience, opportunities arise to express concern and share Christ.

Recreation, arts and crafts, book carts, and music are possible avenues of reaching prisoners. Many will develop a real interest in a new activity because they have nothing else to do. Simple leisure activities may help inmates stay out of trouble in the future in addition to providing an avenue for sharing the gospel with them.

Worship Services and Bible Studies

Many inmates are responsive to the gospel message. They have "hit bottom" and realize acutely their need for God. Worship services and Bible study groups provide an opportunity for sharing the gospel in groups. Contact the chaplain or volunteer coordinator to arrange for services or Bible study groups. Provide Christian literature and individual Bible study workbook materials such as Survival Kits for New Christians or Seekers. Many inmates enjoy cassette tapes of Christian music and teaching.

Correspondence Bible Course

The Home Mission Board offers a free correspondence Bible course through the Evangelism Section. It is a great resource for prisoners. The Home Mission Board receives many letters from persons who have surrendered their lives to Christ as a result of this study. The course is free and lessons are written in easy-to-read style. Order the free pamphlet listed under resources or prisoners may write to Correspondence Bible Course, Evangelism Section, Home Mission Board, 1350 Spring Street, NW, Atlanta, GA 30367, and ask to enroll in lesson one. Persons who write in will be sent an enrollment card along with lesson one.

If you are involved in one-to-one visitation, offer to study along with the prisoner and be an encourager. Get the pamphlet or first lesson for him/her and encourage him or her to enroll.

Supplies for Prison Ministry

Chaplains at prisons and other institutions have a great need for supplies. New boxed Christmas, birthdays, anniversaries, get well, and all occasions cards are appreciated by prisoners who cannot go and purchase these to send to family and friends. Stationary and stamps are also welcomed. Cookies and other baked goods are a treat. Health kits (see p. 39) can be used in prisons. Contact the prison chaplain or volunteer coordinator for a list of needed supplies.

Ministry to Released Offenders

One of the most critical times for a prisoner is when he or she is released. The transition from jail to freedom can be difficult, but volunteers can help smooth the transition time. Volunteers are needed to work with individuals who have shown a desire to change their lives. Sometimes this ministry actually begins before the inmate is released through one-to-one visitation and family ministry.

Following release, volunteers continue to befriend the ex-offender. They help with housing, job hunting, family adjustment, securing appropriate work clothing, medical needs, transportation, and tutoring. It is especially important to include ex-offenders and their families in church activities and to encourage ex-offenders to participate in drug and alcohol programs and support groups, if needed.

To enlist people in this ministry, have one or more persons who are released offenders and are now participating in a church come and speak. Ask the speakers to share what their needs were upon release and how Christian people reached out to them. Ask them to tell how in Christ they found their "new lease on life" and encourage more people to be involved in ministry to released offenders.

Juvenile Rehabilitation

Special care is needed for young offenders, both in and out of detention centers. Establish contact with juvenile court personnel and detention centers to express your interest in working with juvenile offenders. Ministry needs in juvenile facilities are similar to that in adult facilities: tutoring, visitation, leisure activities, Bible studies, and counseling. Sponsors are needed to maintain an ongoing relationship with youth who are in trouble with the law. This may include visiting the youth at home or in the detention center, making court appearances, helping the youth find employment, helping the youth develop positive activities and interests, and being supportive of the family.

Where to Get Additional Help

•Public agencies: Department of Social Services, Police Department, Parole and Probation Office, Criminal Justice System Office
•Local chapters of these organizations: Literacy Council, Salvation Army, Good News Jail and Prison Ministry
•Prison chaplains

Resources

Florida Baptist Convention: "How to Begin Jail and Prison Ministries."

Home Mission Board: "Criminal Justice System" (365-31F); *Ministry/Witness Resource Guide: Jail and Prison* (301-42P); "Correspondence Bible Course" (223-05F).

Buckley, Marie. *Breaking into Prison: A Citizen Guide to Volunteer Action.* Boston: Beacon Press, 1974.

Martin, Sara Hines. *Meeting Needs Through Support Groups.* Birmingham, AL: New Hope, 1992.

RESORT AND LEISURE MINISTRY

Far too often we think of resorts as somewhere else—certainly not places in our community. But tourist attractions, state and local parks, campgrounds, lakes, and rivers are found in many communities. And while we might choose to "go away" for a vacation, relaxation, or fun, others will vacation nearby, and we can minister to them.

Before going further, jot down all the leisure and tourist attractions there are in your community. Include local, county, state, and national parks. Include privately owned facilities. Add museums, monuments, or other places of interest. Add seasonal or annual events such as the county fair, strawberry festival, Octoberfest, Christmas parade,

etc. And don't forget the mall. Many people go shopping as much for entertainment as they do to really purchase something.

Leisure ministries fall into two main categories: ministries at permanent facilities and ministries at temporary events. Ministries at permanent facilities may be done on an ongoing basis or may be one-time projects. Many of the things we might choose to do in other settings will transfer to the leisure or recreational setting giving additional opportunities to use skills in music, drama, crafts, etc.

Seasonal and Special Events

•FAIRS—Arrange to have a booth, display, or place for entertainment at a fair, festival, flea market, etc. If possible, provide a place to sit down. If people have been walking a great deal, they will more likely stop if they can sit down to rest. Children can sit on the floor or ground if an old rug is provided. Folding chairs can be placed around it in a semicircle for adults.

Choose to have a puppet show, mime, music, or other presentation. Keep programs to a maximum of 10 to15 minutes. This is long enough for an adult to rest and is about the limit of the attention span in this type of setting. Include brief presentations of the gospel and at the conclusion, give out pencils, Scripture portions, stickers, etc. Be sure that your church name and number appears on tracts and Scripture portions.

•COLD WATER—Give free cups of cold water in any setting where people are milling around: a fair, flea market, parade, or beach. Include several folding chairs and offer a spot to rest for a few minutes. Use the time to talk and share the gospel. Follow up on any other needs you might learn about in this type of encounter. Provide pencils and forms to complete indicating family or personal needs. Let the person know that your church wants to help. Give a tract or Scripture portion that includes your church name, address, and phone number. This can also be developed into a hot coffee ministry at the mall during the holidays.

•CLOWNING—Clowns or persons dressed in costume can wander through the crowds at a fair, arts and crafts show, festival, parade, or other gathering and talk to people. Families with children are especially responsive. The person in costume can invite people to visit your booth, display, or program at the event. Or clowns can provide an entrée for talking to people using balloons and stickers. Attend a clowning workshop to learn the special skills needed for this type of ministry.

Permanent Facilities

Campgrounds, parks, beaches, hotels, and other tourist attractions provide opportunities for ongoing ministries as well as one-time or short-term projects. Some operate year-round; others will be seasonal only.

People often stay longer at a permanent facility, from several days to a few weeks. There is more time for some relationship building and a greater opportunity to share the gospel.

If there is a campground (public or private) in your area, inquire about providing worship services. Arrange for a place and post information about it around the campground. If it is a Sunday service, hand out fliers on Saturday evening. Include music and a brief message as well as a feature that will appeal to children.

Plan a campfire program with sing-along type music and brief testimonies. In the late afternoon, pass out fliers in the campground inviting folks to attend. Plan for an hour, in 10- to 15-minute segments. People will wander up, stay for a while, and go on. Others will stay for the entire time.

Puppet shows, magic shows, mime, movies, and recreational activities such as volleyball can be used in permanent facilities. Sports clinics, concerts, and community picnics can be used to reach out to people in park settings. Some groups have built small trailers called Good Time Wagons to provide a mobile outdoor base for ministry. These can be used to provide water, carry equipment, be the backdrop for a concert, etc.

Where to Get Additional Help

•FOCAS (Fellowship of Christian Angler's Society), P. O. Box 434, Moraga, CA 94556; (510) 376-8927.
•Campers on Mission, Special Ministries Department, Home Mission Board, 1350 Spring Street, NW, Atlanta, GA 30367. National fellowship of Christian campers.

Resources

•Home Mission Board: *Resort Missions Manual* (364-03P); *Lake Resort Area Manual* (364-67F); *Special Events Manual* (364-71F); *Ministry/Witness Resource Guide: Resort/Leisure* (301-23P).

•Baptist General Convention of Texas: "How to Begin the Church Holiday Hospitality House Program."
•Alban Institute: *Resort Ministries.*

SEAMEN'S MINISTRY

A port ministry is generally led by a missionary or Mission Service Corps director. Because of protocol to be followed when gaining access to ships, this ministry is almost always led by a specially trained staff person. However, there are many ways that volunteers can support this work.

As with Baptist centers and other institutions, collection of needed items is an important, supportive activity. These items are most often needed: clothing, personal care items, health kits, magazines, books, small dictionaries, Bible concordances, calendars, writing paper, envelopes with stamps (overseas rate), Scripture portions, tracts, and cassette tapes.

Christmas Outreach to Seafarers

Prepare and distribute Christmas gifts to seamen. Cookies, scarves, hats, gloves, games, books, and magazines are especially good items.

Winter Clothing Distribution

Because the outside air temperature on northern seas can drop to 40 degrees below zero from December through March, heavy winter clothing is especially appreciated. Heavy winter pants, coats, shoes, socks, and underwear can be distributed to seamen and port personnel.

Bibles

Because seamen come from around the world, a Bible in their native language is often an appreciated gift. Long hours at sea provide time for reading and thinking. Consult with the seamen's ministry director about the purchase of Bibles, New Testaments, or Scripture portions in other languages. These are available from state Bible societies, the American Bible Society, and the International Bible Society.

Outings and Home Visits

Because crew members are not familiar with an area and may not know enough English to feel comfortable asking for directions, outings with volunteers are welcome. Contact the seamen's ministry director about assisting in this way.

Also, let the director know if you would host seamen in your home for a meal, an evening with your family, or at holidays.

Where to Get Additional Help

- Associational director of missions
- Associational church and community ministries director
- State Baptist convention missions director

Resources

Scripture Distribution Office, Home Mission Board, SBC, 1350 Spring Street, NW, Atlanta, GA 30367; (404) 898-7441.

American Bible Society, 1865 Broadway, New York, NY 10023; (212) 408-1499.

Home Mission Board: Seamen's Evangelistic Presentations (12 languages, 12 videos). Order from the Special Ministries Department.

Hunke, Dixie. *Attitudes and Etiquette*. Birmingham, AL. New Hope, 1989.

Snowden, Mark et al. *Meeting the World*. Birmingham, AL: New Hope, 1992.

INTERNATIONAL SEAMEN'S MINISTRIES

Anchorage, Alaska	(907) 338-1425
Baltimore, Maryland	(410) 488-3606
Baton Rouge, Louisiana	(504) 927-6500
Brunswick, Georgia	(912) 267-0631
Burns Harbor, Indiana	(219) 787-8188
Camden, New Jersey	(215) 922-2562
Charleston, South Carolina	(803) 795-0415
Chicago, Illinois	(312) 646-4554
Convent, Louisiana	(504) 562-7196
Everett, Washington	(206) 775-0272
Freeport, Texas	(409) 233-5641
Fort Lauderdale, Florida	(305) 587-8946
Georgetown, South Carolina	(803) 546-4203
Gulfport, Mississippi	(601) 863-1754
Jacksonville, Florida	(904) 633-9971
Lake Charles, Louisiana	(318) 477-1756
Long Beach, California	(213) 432-4920
Los Angeles, California	(213) 432-4920
Mobile, Alabama	(205) 433-7953
New Orleans, Louisiana	(504) 241-7545
Olympia, Washington	(206) 438-0634
Pascagoula, Mississippi	(601) 769-7101
Pensacola, Florida	(904) 434-0243
Philadelphia, Pennsylvania	(215) 922-2562
Port of Astoria, Oregon	(503) 325-7757
Port Royal, South Carolina	(803) 525-0884
Portland, Oregon	(503) 667-8902
Portsmouth, Virginia	(804) 488-1162
Richmond, Virginia	(804) 355-0225
Tampa, Florida	(813) 247-5237
Wilmington, Delaware	(215) 922-2562

SENIOR ADULTS

Contact the Department of Aging in your county to learn how the needs of senior adults are being addressed. You will probably find an array of services from Meals on Wheels to local senior centers. While most of these programs have some paid staff, most use community volunteers to provide the services to the elderly.

Meals on Wheels

This program provides a hot meal daily to senior adults or persons with disabilities who live alone and need assistance to do so. The meals are generally prepared by the county and distributed from senior centers. Volunteers assist with preparing the meals, keeping them hot at the senior center, and preparing them for pickup by the route teams. Volunteers serve in teams of two, one to drive and the other to be the runner and take the meal in.

Meals on Wheels volunteers may sign up to help once a week or once a month. Opportunities abound for witness for the route drivers and runners. Those that have a regular route that they drive at least once a week, get to know the people on the route and become aware of other needs.

Teams can distribute Scripture portions from the American Bible Society at the holidays and other times throughout the year along with the meal.

Tray favors made by children are welcomed by the senior adults. After several weeks of delivering a meal, most people on the route would welcome a visit when the volunteer could come and stay for awhile.

Volunteer Ombudsman/Friendly Visitors

The Department of Aging in most counties provides a variety of services to senior adults whether they live at home, in assisted-living facilities, or in nursing homes. Assisted-living facilities include board and care homes, sheltered homes, and foster care homes. Each provides 24-hour custodial care and some assistance with daily living activities to older citizens who can no longer live alone but who do not require the 24-hour nursing care provided in the nursing home setting.

Friendly Visitors generally receive training from the Department of Aging concerning the special needs of the elderly, applicable laws and regulations, and information about community resources that would be helpful to the senior adult.

Volunteers visit the senior adult in the home, assisted-living facility, or nursing home to provide support, friendship, meaningful one-to-one contact, information, and problem-solving skills. Volunteers are asked to give one hour a week to visit their assigned senior adult. This can be done at a time which will fit in with the volunteer's work and family schedule.

The success of the program lies in making a regular visit. Volunteers are asked to make contact by phone or a card if they have a week they cannot visit. When appropriate the senior adult may be taken shopping, out for lunch or a drive, to church, or wherever they decide.

Friendly Visitors volunteers generally provide a monthly report to the Department of Aging and may contact the department if they have problems or concerns about their assigned senior adult. This is a program which can be done by employed persons, other senior adults, as well as younger people with children. Children can often accompany a parent on a visit as long as the this is agreeable with the senior adult and the Department of Aging.

Telephone Reassurance Program

Trained volunteers provide daily phone contact with elderly persons who live alone 365 days a year. If the senior adult is not reached, a relative, neighbor, friend, or the police is called to check on the person. This is a good ministry for someone who has limited time or does not get out a lot.

Senior Centers

Community-based centers now provide activities and meals for senior adults in most communities. While there are some paid staff members, volunteers are needed. Centers provide cultural and recreational activities, health screenings and information, physical fitness programs, other types of information and referrals, and lunch.

Pets on Wheels

Pets on Wheels is a visitation program that matches volunteer pet owners and their pets with nursing home residents whose activities are limited. There are many nursing home residents who are physically unable to participate in other activities offered by the facility. This program brings the volunteer and his or her pet to the resident to offer cheer and stimulation. Residents who often do not respond to anything else, will respond to a kitten or puppy.

HOP (Helping Older People)

Volunteers help with home repairs, yard work, chores, shopping, and transportation. This can be done by youth and adults together on a regular basis or as a one-time project. Declare a Saturday as HOP Day, and enlist youth and adults for the day. Have projects arranged in advance with specific instructions when the volunteers arrive. This can also be done as a individual or team ministry.

Adult Day Care

An alternative form of care for adults who cannot be left alone during the day is adult day care. This ministry involves a major time commitment, and state regulations must be followed in establishing this service. Guidelines are available regarding staff and facility requirements. Many programs are nonprofit and charge only enough to cover expenses and staff salaries. It is an excellent ministry to families who need assistance in caring for senior adult family members.

Correspondence Bible Course

For persons who find it hard to get out to regular Bible study, the Home Mission Board has developed correspondence Bible study materials. Write to Correspondence Bible Course, Evangelism Section, Home Mission Board, 1350 Spring Street, NW, Atlanta, GA 30367. They will send lesson one and an enrollment card. This is a free, book-by-book study, written in an easy-to-read style. Offer to study with a homebound person and read material aloud if reading has become difficult.

Large-print Resources

One of the common complaints of senior adults is the inability to see small print clearly. This is the result of the eyes losing their elasticity and ability to change focus quickly. It is a normal part of the aging process.

Large-print materials are welcomed by many senior adults. Provide a Bible or a subscription to a magazine such as *Reader's Digest* in large print. Take a senior adult to the library to find large-print materials there in addition to books on cassette tape. Provide a tape recorder, if necessary. Listening to a book on tape can be an enjoyable pastime for someone who likes to read but cannot do it anymore.

SENIOR ADULTS AS VOLUNTEERS

If you are an active senior adult and want to be involved in ministry, there are many opportunities for you. Several service programs have been designed to be staffed by senior adults in particular.

Retired Senior Volunteer Program (RSVP)

Provides senior adults with a variety of opportunities for meaningful service in nonprofit organizations. RSVP places retired people age 60 and over in settings like schools, courts, museums, libraries, and nursing homes. Volunteers serve without pay but in some communities may be reimbursed for transportation and other out-of-pocket expenses.

Foster Grandparents

This program encourages senior adults to serve as volunteers with disadvantaged children who need special care. In some communities low-income senior adults may also earn a small hourly stipend. Foster grandparents help with reading and other basic skills, and provide emotional support to disadvantaged, handicapped, or abused children. Transportation and a hot meal are generally provided. This is a great opportunity for a retired person to minister to a child.

Where to Get Additional Help

•Public agencies: Department of Aging, Department of Social Services, Health Department
•American Association of Retired Persons, 1909 K Street, NW, Washington, DC 20049; (202) 872-4700. (Also contact them for a catalog of publications.)
•National Council on Aging, 600 Maryland Avenue, SW, Washington, DC 20024; (202) 479-1200.
•Alzheimer's Disease and Related Disorders Association, 70 East Lake Street, Suite 600, Chicago, IL 60601; (312) 853-3060.
•Retired Senior Volunteer Program, 1100 Vermont Avenue, NW, Washington, DC; (202) 634-9353.

Resources

Home Mission Board: *Ministry/Witness Resource Guide: Aging* (301-14P); "Beginning Adult Day Care Ministries" (632-20F); "Senior Adults" (365-29F); *Housing for Older Americans* (632-20P).

Alban Institute: Scannell, A. U. *Developing Programs for Older Adults*. Washington, DC: Alban Institute.

Baptist Center for Ethics: *Making Elder Care Decisions*

Baptist Book Store
The Sunday School Providing for Homebound Adults
House, William L. III. *Senior Adult Leaders Notebook*. Nashville: Convention Press.
Kerr, Horace L. *How to Minister to Senior Adults in Your Church*. Nashville: Broadman Press, 1991.
Large-print editions of Christian classics: *Streams in the Desert* (Zondervan); *My Utmost for His Highest* (Revell).

Crichton, Jean. *The Age Care Sourcebook: A Resource Guide for the Aging and Their Families.* New York: A Fireside Book, Simon and Schuster, Inc., 1987.

Gruetzner, Howard. *Alzheimer's: A Caregiver's Guide and Sourcebook.* New York: John Wiley and Sons, Inc., 1988.

Sheridan, Carmel. *Failure-Free Activities for the Alzheimer's Patient: A Guidebook for Caregivers.* San Francisco: Cottage Books, 1987.

Mara, Joy A. *Activities with Impact: Innovative Program Ideas for Adult Housing Residents.* Washington, DC: American Association of Retired Persons, 1987.

McIndoo, Ethel. *Too Late to Say Good-bye* (My Experience with Aging Parents). Birmingham, AL: New Hope, 1988.

SEXUAL ABUSE

Abuse comes in many forms—physical, sexual, verbal, emotional. Often, one form of abuse is coupled with another. Sexual abuse is perpetrated by adults on children, teenagers on children, even children on children, as well as adult on adult or teenager.

Sexual assault crisis centers indicate that rape is the most frequently committed crime in the United States. Although police statistics do not show this, crisis counselors say that for every rape actually reported to the police, 10 are not reported to authorities.

No person asks to be sexually assaulted, either by dress or whereabouts. Although we must caution our children and youth about avoiding clothing and areas that might invite an attack, we must minister to persons who have been victimized in this way, no matter what the circumstances. Rape is a crime of violence. It is traumatic and affects the victim for a lifetime.

Because women and children are most often the victims of sexual assault, this ministry is one that women's organizations need to pursue. Women who have been raped are more comfortable with telling the story to another woman. They need a woman present when the medical exam takes place and when they are being questioned by the police. Christian women are needed to serve as volunteers in sexual assault services programs.

Sexual Assault Crisis Centers and Hotlines

Sexual assault volunteers provide crisis counseling and other services to victims of rape, incest, and other forms of sexual assault at hospitals and police stations. They also provide telephone support as well as companion and advocacy services during medical follow-up and legal proceedings.

Volunteers work directly with victims. Training is required in most programs. Volunteers receive instruction which provides skills in crisis intervention and specialized knowledge of the emotional, medical and legal issues that victims face.

Clerical volunteers are also needed in these programs to help with completing the paper work that must be filed on every victim.

Support Groups

People who have been assaulted recently need a safe place to vent their feelings and receive encouragement from other survivors. Find out if your community offers a support group for victims of sexual assault. Offer to start one, if needed. Discuss format and materials with the staff of a sexual assault crisis center.

Some victims were assaulted as children and must work through the maze of emotions associated with assault that took place years ago. An excellent resource for a support group for persons who have been assaulted is *Meeting Needs Through Support Groups.* This material gives guidelines for leading a support group for persons who have been assaulted.

Where to Get Additional Help

- Police department
- Sexual Assault Crisis Center, Rape Crisis Center
- YMCA Women's Center
- Battered Spouse Shelter
- State Commission for Women

Resources

Snow, Carolyn S. *Abused As a Child: A Christian Student's Response.* Nashville: Convention Press. Educates students about the problems of abuse and equips them to minister to others.

Wright, H. Norman. *Making Peace with Your Past*. Tarrytown, NY: Fleming H. Revell, Co., 1987.

Martin, Sara Hines. *Meeting Needs Through Support Groups*. Birmingham, AL: New Hope, 1992.

Bock, Betty. *You Can Make a Difference*. Birmingham, AL: Woman's Missionary Union, 1992.

Garland, Diana. *Precious in His Sight*. Birmingham, AL: New Hope, 1993.

SOCIAL/MORAL ISSUES

"Somebody really should do something" is said more times than we can count about many issues that face our society. As Christians, we have a responsibility to participate in government and exercise influence to prevent or correct problems and conditions that negatively impact society as a whole. Common social/moral issues that victimize people and must be addressed by concerned citizens include abortion, alcohol and drug abuse, child abuse, criminal justice system reform, ecology, family values, gambling, medical ethics, pornography, poverty, and separation of church and state issues.

Learn the Facts

Before taking a stand on an issue of concern in your community, gather information. Check with your local library. Contact agencies that already deal with this issue. Contact government offices that have brochures and other related information.

Find out about the laws that govern this issue in your community. Talk with persons who enforce these laws. What problems do they see? How could the situation be improved from a law enforcement standpoint? In many situations, laws already exist, but lax enforcement is a contributing factor to the persistence of the problem.

Contact social workers who deal with persons who are victimized by the issue in question. What do they see as a critical area of concern? What suggestions do they have for effecting change?

Contact Local, State, and Federal Government Leaders

Learn the names of those who serve on your city council. Find out who represents your area in county government.

Learn the name of your representative in the state legislature. Often, this person will have a local office as well as an office at the state capitol.

Get the name of your congressional representative as well as your state senators. Your congressional representative will probably have a local office in addition to an office in Washington, D.C.

Express your opinions in writing. Get others to join you in writing public officials. Include your name and return address. Good public officials will respond.

Be brief and to the point when you write. Be sure your facts are accurate. Don't threaten or say anything personally demeaning. Stick to the issue and suggest a specific legislative action.

Take action quickly. When you read newspaper accounts about pending legislation or issues before city or county councils, write immediately. Also, be in contact by letter or phone just before a vote. Many congressional offices will record your opinion about a vote by phone and pass this on to the congressional representative who may be trying to determine how his/her constituency feels about an issue. Here are addresses and phone numbers through which you can express your opinion:

The President
The White House
Washington, DC 20500

White House Comment Line   (202) 456-1111

The Honorable (*your representative*)
United States House of Representatives
Washington, DC 20515

The Honorable (*your senator*)
United States Senate
Washington, DC 20510

Capitol Switchboard   (202) 224-3121

Encourage Responsible Voting

A number of organizations track the voting records of elected officials. Make this information available. Encourage voter registration and participation on election day.

Be aware of the rules regarding nonprofit organizations. Churches may not endorse candidates. However, churches can interview each candidate for an office and present the unedited answer of each candidate to questions. Churches can take stands on issues such as the legalization of gambling and changes in abortion laws.

Economic Action

One of the most powerful tools that we have in this society is the power of the pocketbook. Boycotts can be organized against businesses which advertise in sexually explicit magazines, against companies which advertise during television programs which present questionable moral values, and against companies that sell pornographic materials or serve as outlets for state lotteries.

Write to the president or consumer affairs department of companies in question. Express your opinion. If there is no response, talk with others who share your concerns. As a group, contact the company and let them know that you will no longer be purchasing from them because of their advertising or sales practices.

Keep track of changes in the company position in regard to advertising or sales. If the company makes changes, let them know of your appreciation and willingness to patronize them again.

Raise Awareness

Community apathy about social/moral issues requires an awareness campaign. Plan a presentation or debate about the issue and invite local officials, social workers, or others involved in working with people who have been victimized. Distribute brochures and informational pieces about the issue.

Contact the news media about your presentation. Write letters to the editor about the issue. Prepare feature articles that present information about the target issue.

Get Involved in Advocacy

Persons who need the help of society at large, such as the homeless, often have no one to speak in their behalf. Many of the persons who should be helped by community services and programs are instead victimized by the maze of paperwork and administrative rules. Lack of education and misunderstanding of the agency policies and procedures can make receiving services impossible for some.

Attend public hearings in your community. Attend town hall meetings sponsored by legislators. Ask questions and raise issues that should be addressed.

Get the facts needed to be an advocate for an individual or group. What are the agency rules? How are policies carried out? Who is the specific person that you need to contact? What action needs to be taken? What laws protect the rights of the individual or group?

Develop a plan of action. This may include gathering data, writing letters, visiting officials or agency personnel, taking legal action, or writing editorials and news releases.

Assume that agencies and officials want to do the right thing and will respond to polite, concerned efforts. Don't threaten or take actions that would embarrass a public official (such as contacting the newspaper) until other means of effecting change have been tried. Be persistent in your efforts, polite, but to the point.

Where to Get Additional Help

•Christian Life Commission, 901 Commerce Street, Suite 550, Nashville, TN 37203-3620; (615) 244-2496. You may also call the CLC special message line, (202) 638-4095, to receive information on moral and religious liberty issues in Washington.
•Baptist Joint Committee on Public Affairs, 200 Maryland Avenue, NE, Washington, DC 20002; (202) 544-4226.
•Christian Action Committee or Christian Life Committee of your state Baptist convention.
•American Family Association, P. O. Drawer 2440, Tupelo, MS 38803; (601) 844-5036. Christian organization promoting the biblical ethic of decency in American society with primary emphasis on TV and other media.
•Civic association
•Baptist Center for Ethics, P. O. Box 22188, Nashville, TN 37202; (615) 383-3192

Resources

Garland, Diana. *Precious in His Sight*. Birmingham, AL: New Hope, 1993.

Bock, Betty. *You Can Make a Difference*. Birmingham, AL: Woman's Missionary Union, 1992.

STUDENTS

Once the domain of young Americans, colleges and universities now have students of all ages and ethnic backgrounds. From traditional study programs to adult special interest classes, people are attending school. Of special concern are those students who are away from home. Many are enjoying their independence, but ties with caring persons will ease the transition when difficulties arise. Other students are living at home, working, and going to school, but they still need ministry to their special needs.

Adopt a Student

Befriend a college student. Invite him or her to your home for meals, a place to watch TV, study, or just spend an afternoon or evening with your family. Students who are a long way from home are especially good candidates. Contact a Baptist campus minister or dean of students at college in your area.

If your church has a ministry to college students, talk with students who are already participating. They may be aware of other students who do not attend church anywhere but would be responsive to the invitation of a family in the community.

The Naval Academy in Annapolis, Maryland, has a community sponsorship program for new midshipmen. Sponsors apply during the summer to sponsor a first-year student for one year. However, for many families, the relationship lasts all the way through the four years of school. Primary requirement for this type of sponsorship are lots of food and a willingness to host the student(s) on the weekends. Other schools may have similar programs.

Care Packages

Find out about college students in your community who are attending school locally or away. Prepare "care packages" for them. Include home-baked goodies, Scripture portions, and a copy of *The Student* magazine. If this is a local student, deliver with a note— "Best wishes in your studies, From friends at _____ Baptist Church." If the student is away, mail the package.

College students who are away from home enjoy getting mail, even from folks they don't know. Send cards, holiday items, letters, and care packages to students from your community who are attending school away. Enclose news clippings and items of interest about the community. If possible, try to visit or call the student when he or she is at home.

The Student Magazine

Provide subscriptions to *The Student* for college students from your community. Articles examine issues that are important to students as well as collegiate Bible study material. Call the customer service center 1 (800) 458-2772 to order or use the Dated Literature Order Form from the Baptist Sunday School Board.

Collegiate Bible Study

Host a regular Bible study for students in your home. Provide transportation and refreshments. Or arrange to have a campus Bible study in a dorm or empty classroom. Choose material that examines what the Bible says about issues of importance to students.

Exam Week

In her book *Count It All Joy*, Barbara Joiner describes Cookie Crumble, a ministry to international students at the University of Montevallo. It is a ministry that could be duplicated by organizations and churches across the country.

Obtain a list of foreign students at a college or university in your community. Find out the dates of exam week. Start baking and freezing cookies well in advance so that you will have enough to deliver during exam week. Get two- to three-pound coffee cans and decoupage or decorate them with Christmas paper. Contact the American Bible Society to obtain Bibles in the languages of the students.

At the beginning of exam week, start delivering. Enlist an international student to help you find your way to the dorms and to meet students. Include a message saying that this is a gift from friends at _____ Baptist Church. Include your phone number and indicate that if students need help, want to talk, or need a place to stay during the holidays, they should contact this number. Be prepared to minister.

Friendship International House

During the days between Christmas and New Year's Day, college dormitories close and many international students have no place to go. Friendship International House is a program designed to meet that need and also give international students the opportunity to visit in an American home. (For a complete description of FIH, see p. 34.)

Where to Get Additional Help

•Chaplain, campus minister, or dean of students at local college or university
•Student Ministry Department, MSN 153, Baptist Sunday School Board, 127 Ninth Avenue, North, Nashville, TN 37234
•State student director/director of campus ministries
•Associational director of missions

Resources

Baptist Book Store
Ministering to Students Through the Church
Spending a Life: Materialism or Sacrifice
Beautiful Originals Versus Bad Copies
Confronting Racism

Hunke, Dixie. *Attitudes and Etiquette*. Birmingham, AL: New Hope, 1989.

Snowden, Mark et al. *Meeting the World*. Birmingham, AL: New Hope, 1992.

TRAVELERS/TRUCK STOP MINISTRY

At any time of the day or night, any day of the year, people are traveling, some for work, some for leisure, others in transition of some kind. And invariably, they have needs which can be met.

Truck Stops

Because truck stops are in business to make a profit, you must take care in the types of activities selected. For instance, a truck stop would not want you to give away coffee, cold beverages, or snacks because they are selling these items. Permission from the management must be obtained for any activity.

A good ongoing ministry in a truck stop or tourist information center is a tract/literature rack. Keep this stocked with Scripture portions, magazines, tracts, and information about where to call for assistance. Also provide information about local church services.

Develop a good relationship with the truck-stop manager and offer to provide a Sunday or week-night worship service. This type of ministry is best done by teams or couples.

Audiotape Lending Library

Establish a lending library at a local truck stop. Include tapes with Christian Bible study, music, and family enrichment as well as tapes on stress, money management, and self-esteem. Work out a system for checking out and returning tapes. Many drivers run the same route frequently and would enjoy borrowing tapes.

Include information for returning tapes by mail. This ministry could be expanded to families in your community who would like to borrow tapes to listen to on trips or while commuting. Public libraries have novels and self-improvement tapes but only a limited supply of Christian tapes.

Do not reproduce tapes with copyrighted material.

Assistance to Travelers

Volunteer to help with an ongoing ministry to travelers in your area. Many communities have nonprofit, interdenominational, or nonsectarian programs to assist travelers. These run information booths in airport and bus terminals and provide information as well as referrals to social service agencies as needed.

Or volunteer to help with the local chamber of commerce or tourist information booth. Provide a list of area churches and ministries to the chamber of commerce or tourist information bureau to be given to visitors and newcomers.

Other Ministries to Travelers

•Set up a free coffee stand at a highway rest area or waiting area of an airport, bus terminal, or train station. (You will want to contact the management for permission to serve.)
•Sponsor a first-aid station at a rest area or service station.
•Post a list of churches which provide help to travelers.
•Place Christian literature and Scripture portions in waiting areas such as airports, bus terminals, and train stations.
•Set up a large cooler with fresh cold water at a highway rest stop. Offer free cups of cold water to travelers. Have Scripture portions and/or New Testaments to give away.
•Sponsor a free car wash and/or vacuum service for travelers. Eating in the car helps pass the time when traveling but leaves a mess. Many people try to clean out their cars a bit at rest stops. Arrange a free vacuum service. Give out tracts or Scripture portions.
•Distribute travel kits at rest areas or truck stops to persons who need personal items but cannot afford them. If there is a chaplain, work with him to distribute kits and/or talk with management about the need. Include soap, washcloth, razor, toothbrush, toothpaste, and a tract or Scripture portion.

Where to Get Additional Help

•Travelers Aid Society, Salvation Army, homeless shelter.
•State convention and associational church and community ministries directors

Resources

Home Mission Board: Schlegel, Sam, and Betty Anne Schlegel. *Truck Stop Ministry Manual* (631-101F).

UNEMPLOYED

Unemployment places a tremendous financial and emotional burden on families. Ministry to unemployed persons, both to the chronically unemployed and those who are out of work due to recession or other factors, can be an important community ministry.

Support Group

Form a support group for unemployed persons. This type of group needs to allow participants a safe place to talk about how they are feeling. Many times unemployed persons hide their fears and disappointments from their families. This ministry encourages others. Like other support groups, participants share their coping strategies and pray together.

Résumé Preparation

Because an unemployed person likely has financial difficulties, he may not be able to afford professional résumé preparation services. Enlist persons with word processing skills to help the unemployed with résumé preparation. There are many books available from the library to help develop good résumés.

Job Skills

Offer classes in basic skills such as typing or word processing. If an unemployed person needs to complete high school, help prepare for the GED (General Education Diploma) test.

Some people need to learn how to fill out a job application. Most companies want the prospective employee to complete the application immediately. Some unemployed persons need help in understanding what types of information they need to have with them in order to adequately complete an application. Help the unemployed person put together a file of information including complete names, addresses, and phone numbers of previous employers; employment dates, supervisors, and descriptions of work done for previous employers; current job skills; and references' names, addresses, and phone numbers.

Teach interviewing skills. Hold mock interviews and videotape or record the candidate. Then watch or listen to the tape together and discuss ways to improve.

Clothes Closet

Establish a special clothes closet for the unemployed that includes clothing suitable for job interviews. Provide guidelines about appropriate dress, makeup, and hairstyles. Give tips for making a good first impression.

Supportive Services

During periods of unemployment, a family may need help with food, clothing, rent or mortgage, utility payments, medical care, and transportation. Determine what services your congregation can provide. Learn about resources in your community. Assist unemployed persons in fully utilizing community resources that will help them through this time. Encourage them to volunteer and use their time productively in spite of being unemployed. Community service as a volunteer often leads to employment, can provide an opportunity to learn new skills, and help the unemployed person maintain a positive attitude.

Where to Get Additional Help

•Public agencies: Department of Social Services, Unemployment Office, State Employment Service
•YWCA: Help for Displaced Homemakers program
•Associational church and community ministries director

Resources

Unemployed/Unfulfilled. Serendipity Support Group Series. Serendipity House Bible study. Useful as the basis for a weekly Bible study and support group for the unemployed.

Martin, Sara Hines. *Meeting Needs Through Support Groups*. Birmingham, AL: New Hope, 1992.

4

COMMUNITY MINISTRY AND THE NEXT GENERATION

Think back to your own childhood. How did you learn to be concerned for other people? Most of us can remember a particular caring person who influenced us or a parent or teacher who got us involved in ministry. Children still learn to care by modeling the actions of adults. We must involve preschoolers, children, and youth in ministry in order to teach them how to be caring people. Their involvement in community ministry now will influence them for the rest of their lives.

Because we sometimes tend to think of children as miniature adults, it is helpful to periodically remind ourselves of their developmental characteristics. This will assist us in planning ministry projects and activities that are age appropriate. Most youth and children's missions organizations have materials related to the characteristics of each age group that are very helpful. Both new and experienced leaders need to periodically review these developmental characteristics.

The best ministry projects are those that are an outgrowth of study. This reinforces learning and helps children/youth see that what they learn in missions organizations applies to real life. If possible, then, choose projects that tie in with your current unit of study and meet needs in your community. If the current unit does not naturally lend itself to follow up through a ministry project, use other resources to get ideas.

If you need to contact an agency representative (such as the activities director at a nursing home), do so before sharing the project idea with your children. Don't get them excited about a project and then have to tell them they can't do it.

It is fine to have a general discussion about ministry with your group and have them name off ideas for ministry. Based on the list they make, tell them you will check into the possibilities of carrying out an idea. Then report back in another session. If a project cannot be done, explain why. But again, don't start the actual planning process with the kids unless you know it can be done.

Next, plan the project. Use the ministry plan sheet included in this book. A plan sheet helps you remember to cover all the details. Most bad experiences in community ministry are the result of poor planning.

Train the group. Be sure children or youth know what to expect. Practice skills needed for the ministry.

Lead the ministry project. The old saying, Plan your work, and work your plan still holds true. But, be flexible. Have an alternate activity ready if possible.

Evaluate. Immediately after the ministry project, take the group for sodas and talk about the experience. Later, include a written evaluation with your ministry plan sheet. Keep a file of these sheets and other pertinent information. You will find this a most helpful reference.

Choosing Ministry Projects for Children and Youth

Ministry projects should meet a real need. Teach kids that helping people is more important than getting credit or recognition for a project.

Ministry projects should allow the children to participate directly whenever possible. Collecting or making items to send to a nursing home, shelter, or Baptist center is good, but the children will learn more if they have personal contact. For example, if you are making tray cards for the nursing home, let the kids visit and deliver them.

MINISTRY IDEAS FOR CHILDREN AND YOUTH
Nursing home
Share a Toy
Adopt a Grandparent
Safe Halloween (visiting residents in costume)
Old-fashioned games
Easter egg hunt
Intergenerational choir
Pool party
Transportation volunteers (youth)
Musical programs
Collecting and delivering personal items

Migrant/Seaman/Prison Ministry
Preparing health kits
Bible school for migrant children (youth)

Elderly/Persons with Disabilities in the Community
Yard work
Making or delivering cards or artwork

Errands (youth)
Deliver decorated Christmas trees
Visitation
Giving large-print Bibles or hymnbook
Reading aloud
Helping with hobbies
Delivering church service tapes

Collection Ministries
Food—for food pantry/shelter/Baptist center
Personal items—for shelter/Baptist center/nursing home
Clothing—for crisis closet, needy child
Magazines, Christian literature—for laundromats, hospitals, and other waiting areas

Internationals
Invite to home/church.
Provide appropriate Scripture portions.
Give small gifts.
Take sight-seeing.

Military/Others Who Are Away from Home
Send letters and cards, small gifts, magazines, newspapers, or books.
Make and send cookies.
Make and send tapes of church services.

Nonreaders
Make flash cards, charts, or picture files for those who teach.
Tutor a first- or second-grader.
Provide Bibles/Scripture portions in simple English.
Sponsor trips to the library for children from disadvantaged homes. Attend storytime together.

Children
Youth-led Backyard Bible Clubs.

Baby-sitting Service/Parent's Night Out/Mom's Morning Out—Youth provide group child care at the church, adult-supervised. This could be done in conjunction with another ministry of the church such as a literacy class.

Youth adopt a child to befriend that does not have a big brother or sister.

Christmas event planned and led by youth for neighborhood children. Each child brings a toy to share with a needy family. Or each child brings a children's book to share. These can be given to needy families or to the literacy council.

Christmas Gifts for Needy Children—Youth purchase, wrap, and deliver.

Mitten or Sock Tree—Set up a tree branch in a stand. Invite children and youth to bring mittens, gloves, or socks to hang on the tree. When the tree is full, deliver to a homeless shelter.

Easter Baskets for Children Living in a Shelter—Fill with candy and a tract telling the true meaning of Easter.

Friendship Box—Fill a box with items for a needy child or family. Include toiletries, books, and small toys.

Book Drive for a Prison—Obtain copies of paperback novels, assorted magazines, and other reading material. Include Christian literature, but do not limit the collection to Bibles. Deliver to the prison chaplain for distribution.

Resources

Ellis, Susan, Anne Weisbard, and Katherine Noyes. *Children As Volunteers: Preparing for Community Service, revised edition*. Philadelphia: Energize, Inc., 1991.

Bolton, Joy Luebbert. *Ideas for Nursing Home Ministries*. Birmingham: Woman's Missionary Union, 1990. Chapter 7, "Children and Youth," has guidelines, ministry ideas, and tips for visiting a nursing home with preschoolers and elementary school children.

Campolos, Anthony. *Ideas for Social Action: A Handbook on Mission and Service for Christian Young People*. Grand Rapids: Zondervan Publishing Corp., 1983.

Smith, Anne. *Get into the Action*. Birmingham, AL: Woman's Missionary Union, 1990.

Stubblefield, Jerry. *Missions Activities for Men and Boys*. Memphis: Brotherhood Commission, 1987.

PLAN SHEET FOR COMMUNITY MINISTRY

Project or Ongoing Ministry ____

Purpose of Project of Ministry ____

Date _______________________Time _________________________Place _______________________

Target group or issue _________________Contact Person _________________Phone __________

Training needed by participants, how training will be given _______________________________

____

Planning and work to be done in advance   Person responsible Phone

_____________________________________ _______________ _____________

_____________________________________ _______________ _____________

_____________________________________ _______________ _____________

_____________________________________ _______________ _____________

Supplies or Materials Needed   To be supplied by

_____________________________________ _______________________

_____________________________________ _______________________

_____________________________________ _______________________

_____________________________________ _______________________

Work to be done during community ministry activity Persons assigned Phone

_____________________________________ _______________ _____________

_____________________________________ _______________ _____________

_____________________________________ _______________ _____________

Witnessing opportunities anticipated ____

____

Transportation needed ____

____

Budget expenditures ____

Evaluation ____

____

COMMUNITY MINISTRY SKILLS INVENTORY

Please check your skills that could be used in community ministry in an emergency situation or on an ongoing basis.

_ Accounting
_ Administrative assistant
_ Administrator
_ Advocate for handicap
_ Artist
_ Auto care—outside
_ Auto mechanic—general
_ Auto mechanic—full

_ Baby care (prenatal–18 months)
_ Baby-sitting
_ Backhoe operator
_ Baking
_ Banking process
_ Barbering
_ Bargain shopping
_ Bartering
_ Beautician
_ Bedside manners
_ Bicycle repair
_ Birth control education
_ Bread baking
_ Brick and block layer
_ Budget establishment
_ Building construction skills

_ Cake decorator
_ Camp counselor
_ Canning process
_ Carpentry—minor
_ Carpentry—skilled
_ Changing fuses
_ Child care
_ Claims representative for Social Security Administration
_ Cleaning
_ Clerk
_ Clothing sorter
_ Clothing supplier
_ Coaching sports
_ Communication specialist
_ Computer operator
_ Computer system setup
_ Concrete finisher
_ Cooking
_ Co-op functions
_ Counseling
_ Crane operator
_ Crocheting
_ Cross-stitching
_ Creative dance
_ Creative writing
_ Curtain hanging
_ Cutting grass

_ Data processing
_ Decorating
_ Design—layout
_ Dishwasher
_ Door framing/hanging
_ Drain cleaning
_ Drama (acting)
_ Dressing changes
_ Driving
_ Drywall work

_ Editor
_ Electrical appliance repair
_ Electronics equip. repair
_ Electronics equipment operation
_ Elderly care
_ Embroidery
_ Emergency transportation
_ Encourager
_ Exercise routines

_ Farm skills
_ Financial systems
_ Finish trim (carpentry)
_ Fishing information
_ Flower gardens
_ Flower arrangement
_ Framing walls
_ French language

_ Garage doors—install/service
_ Gardening
_ German language
_ General manager
_ Gourmet food
_ Government accounting
_ Graphic design
_ Grass cutting
_ Greek language
_ Grocery shopping with women
_ Guitar playing

_ Hair stylist
_ Handicap services
_ Hand tool skills
_ Hanging insulation
_ Health care
_ Heavy equipment operator
_ Helper
  Homemaking skills
_ Home economics
_ Home improvement
_ Home repair (minor)

_ Hospital visitation
_ Housecleaning
_ House-sitting

_ Income-tax preparation
_ Injections (medicines)
_ Insurance field
_ Interior remodeling

_ Janitorial skills

_ Key punch operator
_ Knitting

_ Laborer
_ Library skills teacher
_ Library tours
_ Lock installation
_ Lock repair

_ Macramé
_ Masonry work
_ Math instruction
_ Meals for elderly
_ Meal planning
_ Media
_ Mending
_ Mentally ill care
_ Midwife

_ Natural childbirth methods teacher
_ Navy medic
_ Nurse—general
_ Nurse—cardiac care
_ Nurse—geriatric care
_ Nurse—home care
_ Nurse—pediatric care
_ Nurse—respiratory care

_ Nutrition

_ Office assistant
_ Organic gardening
_ Organizer

_ Painting
_ Parenting skills
_ Pets on Wheels
_ Piano playing
_ Pilot
_ Photography
_ Physical labor
_ Physical therapy
_ Plumbing
_ Power tool skills

_ Public speaking
_ Puppeteering

_ Rake leaves
_ Reading to others
_ Reupholstery
_ Resume preparation
_ Roofing
_ Russian language

_ Sales experience
_ Seamstress
_ Secretarial skills
_ Sewing
_ Sheet rock work
_ Shelter overnight
_ Shorthand
_ Sign language
_ Small business operation
_ Spackling
_ Spanish language
_ Sports activities

_ Teaching
   _ Childbirth preparation and newborn care
   _ Cooking
   _ GED preparation
   _ Guitar
   _ Life skills
   _ Music
   _ Sewing
_ Teen activities
_ Telephone repair or installation
_ Terminally ill care
_ Transportation—car
_ Transportation—van
_ Transportation—bus
_ Truck driver
_ Tutoring
   _ Math
   _ English
_ Typing

_ Welding
_ Window replacement
_ Winterization
_ Woodworking skills
_ Word processing
_ Writer

_ Yard work

_ Other:

Name ____

Address ____

City, State, ZIP ____

Phone (Home) _______________________________ Phone (Work) _________________________

Please add any other information about areas of service in community ministry on the back of this form.

My friend/spouse may also be interested. Name ____________________________________ Phone ___________

TEACHING GUIDE

Two and one-half hours class time is required to receive Church Study Course credit for this book. In addition to participating in class activities and discussion, each person must also read the book. If the book is taught in one session, schedule 3 hours to allow time for a break.

PREPARING TO TEACH

1. Thoroughly study this book.

2. Secure name tags, paper, pencils (step 10), and current newspapers (step 14) for all learners.

3. If each attender will not have a copy of the book, arrange for them to purchase one prior to the beginning of the class.

4. Display suggested resources and if possible arrange for them to be sold before or after the conference.

5. Duplicate enough copies of the "Community Ministry Skills Inventory" (p. 69), the "Plan Sheet for Community Ministry" (p. 68), and the evaluation questions from the personal learning activities (p. 71) for each person to have a copy.

6. Prepare or ask someone who will be attending to prepare a 3- to 5-minute devotion on Why Do Community Ministry? Suggest using Matthew 25:35ff. for the biblical basis.

7. Arrange for refreshments during the break.

8. Have a chalkboard or large sheets of paper ready for use in steps 14 and 18.

9. If you are teaching a group of WMU members, plan to call attention to "A Special Word to WMU Members" in the personal learning activities (p. 72). If possible, secure the name, address, and telephone number of the closest church and community ministries director.

STEPS TO TEACHING

INTRODUCTORY ACTIVITY

10. As learners arrive, give each one a name tag. Ask them to write their names on one side of the tag and a hobby or skill on the other side. After a few minutes, have conferees introduce themselves to one other person in the room by sharing their names and what they have written. (10 min.)

11. Bring the group back together by saying that who you are is an important resource for meeting community needs! Briefly overview the conference. (5 min.)

BIBLICAL BASIS

12. Share the devotion Why Do Community Ministry? Have prayer. (5 min.)

13. Ask conferees to discuss who should do community ministry. Share that if you have the ability or resource to meet a need, you are called to minister. Explain that ministry takes place when abilities or resources are used to meet needs. (5 min.)

DETERMINE NEEDS

14. Members will work individually and in groups of four. Each person will need at least one section of a current newspaper. Instruct learners to scan the paper for articles, advertisements, or announcements related to needs in the community. Have each person compile a list of needs. Once everyone has had time to complete their lists, compile the results into one master list. From the master list, ask each group to select three needs it considers to be the most important to be met. Ask one person from each group to write the group's top three needs on a large sheet of paper or on the chalkboard. (20 min.)

15. Review the list of needs and as a large group select the top five needs which should be addressed in your community. If people are present from different communities, have each community select five needs. (10 min.)

DISCOVER RESOURCES

16. Share with your learners that they are a resource to meet a need. Have each person turn to page 2 in his or her book and answer the first six questions under "Witnessing Through Community Ministry." (5 min.)

17. Distribute copies of the "Community Ministry Skills Inventory" to each person. Ask each person to use the skills listed as ideas for writing a list of all the things they have done that might be used in a ministry situation. After they have completed their lists, have them circle or highlight those things which they are willing to do now. (15 min.)

The break will begin as each person finishes this activity. Suggest that conferees look at the display of resources during this time.

PLANNING A MINISTRY

18. Ask conferees to again work in their small groups. Using the index on page 73 of the book, ask persons to identify possible ministries to meet each of the top five needs. If you have a large number of groups, be prepared to assign each one a section of

the index to work with such as ministries listed in A-D, E-H, I-K, etc. Allow each group to report, recording possible ministries next to the needs of the group list. (20 min.)

19. Have each person identify an ability he or she has that could be used in one of the selected ministries. (5 min.)

20. Distribute copies of the "Plan Sheet for Community Ministry." If persons who will be conducting a ministry as a group are attending, have them work together. Have others work in groups of four. Using the identified top five needs and possible ministries, have each group select one possible project and complete the plan sheet for that project. (20 min.)

21. Have each group discuss how it would now implement its ministry. Suggest that groups scan the first two chapters in the book for help. (15 min.)

EVALUATION

22. Discuss the importance of evaluations. They show what has been done right as well as what can be improved on. Using the completed plan sheets, have each group discuss when and how it would evaluate its project. Distribute questions from the personal learning activities and suggest they be used as a guide for planning evaluation.
(10 min.)

COMMITMENT (5 MIN.)

23. Share the section "Personal Satisfaction" on page 5.

24. Challenge each conferee to sign and date the cover of his or her book as a reminder of the commitment to become involved and involve others in community ministry. Close with a time of prayer.

PERSONAL LEARNING ACTIVITIES

Good for you! By opening this book, you have taken the first step toward involvement in community ministry. These personal learning activities will guide you in identifying "your" ministry. As you read and as you work through selected activities, ask God to show you His plan for ministry in your community.

One of my favorite truths is that If you have the ability or resource to meet a need, then you are called to minister. I believe that Jesus teaches us by His example and by His words that we are to be actively involved in our communities meeting needs, and by doing so opening doors to share the good news. Your journey toward community ministry is threefold: (1) discovering needs, (2) discovering resources, and (3) matching needs with resources in order for ministry to take place.

YOUR COMMUNITY

Human need is all around you, but it is often easier to recognize needs across town, across the country, or across the globe than across the street.

The author writes that this is a book about "backyards." Take time to define your backyard by writing down the answers to these questions:
- •What is your backyard? What are the boundaries? What is in your backyard? How did you decide these things?
- •How does your backyard look? What does how it looks say about it? What would you like to change? Why?
- •Who lives in your backyard? What would you like to know about your backyard that you don't already know?
- •What needs do you know of that exist in your backyard? What is being done to meet them? Which needs are going unmet? Now think about the community around your church. Answer the same questions for the church's backyard.
- •How do you feel about the needs in your community? Stop and pray and tell God how you feel. Ask Him to be your guide as you discover what needs to be done and what He wants you to do!

Choose at least one of the following activities to further help you discover needs in your community.

Windshield survey

If you had difficulty answering the questions about your backyard, or if you are new to your community, you may choose to take a windshield survey. Drive slowly through the area you defined as your (or your church's) backyard. Look for things you have not noticed before. When you get home, write down your observations and the needs you may have "discovered."

Change your routine

Do you always drive or walk to familiar places along the same route? It's an easy habit to develop. For a few days take different routes to church, work, school, or shopping. Look for new things about your community. Did you see indications of needs that you weren't aware of? What were they? Write down your observations.

Newsworthy observations

Sit down with a current newspaper and open this book to the index. As you scan the articles, advertisements, and announcements, make a list of the needs you read about. Look back over the needs you have identified and match them with possible ministries listed in the index. Note any ministries already taking place in your community.

Mapping your community

On a map of your community, mark your home and your church. Next mark areas or places where you have discovered needs. What does this say about your community? If necessary, rewrite your description of your backyard.

YOUR RESOURCES

Your availability, abilities, interests, hobbies, and experiences are resources for meeting needs. These activities will help you discover and affirm what your resources are!

Turn to the "Community Ministry Skills Inventory" on page 69 of your book. Use the skills listed as a resource for writing a list of all the things you have done that might be used in a ministry situation. After you have completed your list, circle or highlight those things you are willing to do now.

Answer these questions also found on page 2 of your book:
- What are my personal interests and skills?
- What would I like to accomplish through community ministry?
- What age group do I want to work with?
- Do I prefer to work alone or in a group?
- What kind of time commitment can I make?
- Do I want to work directly with persons in need, or would I prefer a behind-the scenes ministry?

YOUR MINISTRY

As an introductory activity to discovering your ministry, review your responses to the exercises you have completed. What need or needs would you like to help meet? Write a specific service expectation for the ministry you think you would like to do.

Contact a community ministry center or social service agency and let the volunteer coordinator know of your interest. If their agency needs match your abilities and availability, congratulations, you have discovered your community ministry!

If you are beginning a ministry either as a individual or as a group, complete the "Plan Sheet for Community Ministry" on page 68. Share your plans with the person(s) to whom you will be accountable.

Plan your evaluation of the project. Evaluations show what has been done right as well as what can be improved on. Use these questions as a guide for your evaluation.
- Was the purpose accomplished?
- Were the plans adequate? Should anything else have been included?
- Was the preparation adequate? Could it have been improved?
- Were there problems? How were they handled? What did you learn from them?
- Could further training or additional resources have been used?
- What evidence of spiritual growth was seen in the persons helped? the helpers?
- What important relationships were established?
- How was verbal witness a part of the project?
- Has this ministry run its course?
- What happens next?

OPTIONAL ACTIVITIES

Secure a copy of the *Church/Community Needs Survey Guide* from the Home Mission Board (1 [800] 634-2462) and conduct the survey with whomever will be involved in the community ministry.

Read one of the suggested resources for the area of need you have chosen for your ministry.

A SPECIAL WORD TO WMU MEMBERS

As you become involved in meeting needs in your community, whether by yourself or with a group, please communicate with the person in your association or state who has the responsibility for church and community ministries. You may be the answer to one of this person's prayers for beginning or expanding a ministry; or you may be needed to make a special contribution to an existing ministry.

"Expect great things from God, attempt great things for God."—William Carey

About the teaching guide author

For 15 years Trudy Johnson served as a home missionary in the area of church and community ministries. In 1991 she joined the national Woman's Missionary Union staff as Missions Involvement specialist. She has written the "Hope for Hurting Humanity" *A Guide for Planning and Conducting Ministry and Witness Projects in Your Church* and coauthored *The Son! His Redemptive Sacrifice* and *Holy Spirit! His Redemptive Force!* Facilitator Guides. In addition, she has written for numerous WMU and Sunday School Board publications and been featured in Home Mission Board videos and their *MissionsUSA* magazine. Trudy is a member of the International Platform Association and also listed in *Who's Who Worldwide*. A popular speaker, conference leader, and teacher, Trudy lives in Birmingham with her son A. J. and her mother.

Helpful Resource Information

The Alban Institute, 4125 Nebraska Avenue, NW, Washington, DC 21106; 1 (800) 457-2674 (ordering); 1 (800) 242-5226 (consulting).

American Bible Society, 1865 Broadway, New York, NY 10023; (212) 408-1200.

Baptist Sunday School Board, 127 Ninth Avenue, North, Nashville, TN 37234; (615) 251-2783.

Baptist Center for Ethics, P. O. Box 22188, Nashville, TN 37202; (615) 383-3192.

Baptist General Convention of Texas, 333 North Washington, Dallas, TX 75246-1798; (214) 828-5100.

Brotherhood Commission, 1548 Poplar Avenue, Memphis, TN 38104; 1 (800) 727-6466.

Christian Life Commission, 901 Commerce Street, Suite 550, Nashville, TN 37203-3620; (615) 244-2495.

Florida Baptist Convention, 1230 Hendricks Avenue, Jacksonville, FL 32207; (904) 396-2351.

Home Mission Board, 1350 Spring Street, NW, Atlanta, GA 30367; 1 (800) 634-2642.

New Hope, P. O. Box 12065, Birmingham, AL 35202-2065; (205) 991-4933.

Woman's Missionary Union, P. O. Box 830010, Birmingham, AL 35283-0010; (205) 991-4933.

World Changers Resources, P. O. Box 830010, Birmingham, AL 35283-0010; (205) 991-4933.

Baptist Book Stores carry many of the books cited as resources throughout this book. For the Baptist Book Store nearest you, contact the Customer Service Center at 1 (800) 458-2772; or for western states, 1 (800) 677-7797.

Requirements for Church Study Course Credit

Ideas for Community Ministries is course number 03-350 in the subject area Christian Growth and Service.

Credit for the course may be obtained in two ways: (1) conference or class—read the book and participate in a 2½-hour study; (2) individual study—read the book, do the personal learning activities, and have a church leader check written work.

Request credit on Form 725, "Church Study Course Enrollment/Credit Request," (revised) available from the Church Study Course Awards Office, 127 Ninth Avenue, North, Nashville, TN 37234.

Complete details about the Church Study Course system, courses available, and diplomas offered is in the *Church Study Course Catalog* available from the church office or Awards Office.

About the author

Joy Bolton, a native of New Orleans, Louisiana, graduated from Mississippi College with a bachelor's degree in music education in 1975. She completed the master of church music degree at Southern Baptist Theological Seminary in 1978.

Joy has served as church WMU director, associational WMU director, and on the state WMU council in Pennsylvania. She has written for WMU publications since 1979. She wrote three of the service plans in the book *Creative Installation Services;* she also wrote *Ideas for Nursing Home Ministries.*

Joy's husband, Lee, pastors First Baptist Church of Eastport in Annapolis, Maryland. They began their ministry there in January 1990 after serving over seven years in Reading, Pennsylvania. They have two children, Carol and Roscoe.